Speeches

On Religion and Politics, Including the Address to Parliament

Swami Vivekananda

Institute of Thought & Philosophy

GRAPEVINE INDIA

Published by

GRAPEVINE INDIA PUBLISHERS PVT LTD

www.grapevineindia.com
Delhi | Mumbai
email: grapevineindiapublishers@gmail.com

Ordering Information:
Quantity sales: Special discounts are available on quantity purchases by corporations, associations, and others.
For details, reach out to the publisher.

First published by Grapevine India 2024

The mission of the Institute of Thought and Philosophy is to preserve and propagate the teachings of Swami Vivekananda. This great Indian spiritual leader is known for introducing the West to Hinduism. Drawing from his vast literary legacy, we provide valuable insights and practical guidance for modern living.

Have any query or feedback? Please reach out to us at
ITPPress123@gmail.com

FIRST PUBLIC LECTURE IN THE EAST

(Delivered in Colombo)

After his memorable work in the West, Swami Vivekananda landed at Colombo on the afternoon of January 15, 1897, and was given a right royal reception by the Hindu community there. The following address of welcome was then presented to him:

SRIMAT VIVEKANANDA SWAMI

REVERED SIR,

In pursuance of a resolution passed at a public meeting of the Hindus of the city of Colombo, we beg to offer you a hearty welcome to this Island. We deem it a privilege to be the first to welcome you on your return home from your great mission in the West.

We have watched with joy and thankfulness the success with which the mission has, under God's blessing, been crowned. You have proclaimed to the nations of Europe and America the Hindu ideal of a universal religion, harmonising all creeds, providing spiritual food for each soul according to its needs, and lovingly drawing it unto God. You have preached the Truth and the Way, taught from remote ages by a succession of Masters whose blessed feet have walked and sanctified the soil of India, and whose gracious presence and inspiration have made her, through all her vicissitudes, the Light of the World.

To the inspiration of such a Master, Shri Ramakrishna Paramahamsa Deva, and to your self-sacrificing zeal, Western nations owe the priceless boon of being placed in living contact with the spiritual genius of India, while to many of our own countrymen, delivered from the glamour of Western civilisation, the value of Our glorious heritage has been brought home.

By your noble work and example you have laid humanity under an obligation difficult to repay, and you have shed fresh lustre upon our Motherland. We pray that the grace of God may continue to prosper you and your work, and

We remain, Revered Sir,

Yours faithfully,

for and on behalf of the Hindus of Colombo,

P. COOMARA SWAMY,

Member of the Legislative Council of Ceylon,

Chairman of the Meeting.

A. KULAVEERASINGHAM, Secretary .

Colombo, January, 1897 .

The Swami gave a brief reply, expressing his appreciation of the kind welcome he had received. He took advantage of the opportunity to point out that the demonstration had not been made in honour of a great politician, or a great soldier, or a millionaire, but of a begging Sannyâsin, showing the tendency of the Hindu mind towards religion. He urged the necessity of keeping religion as the backbone of the national life if the nation were to live, and disclaimed any personal character for the welcome he had received, but insisted upon its being the recognition of a principle.

On the evening of the 16th the Swami gave the following public lecture in the Floral Hall:

What little work has been done by me has not been from any inherent power that resides in me, but from the cheers, the goodwill, the blessings that have followed my path in the West from this our very beloved, most sacred, dear Motherland. Some good has been done, no doubt, in the West, but specially to myself; for what before was the result of an emotional nature, perhaps, has gained the certainty of conviction and attained the power and strength of demonstration. Formerly I thought as every Hindu thinks, and as the Hon. President has just pointed out to you, that this is the Punya Bhumi, the land of Karma. Today I stand here and say, with the conviction of truth, that it is so. If there is any land on this earth that can lay claim to be the blessed Punya Bhumi, to be the land to which all souls on this earth must come to account for Karma, the land to which every soul that is wending its way Godward must come to attain its last home, the land where humanity has attained its highest towards gentleness, towards generosity, towards purity, towards calmness, above all, the land of introspection and of spirituality — it is India. Hence have started the founders of religions from the most ancient times, deluging the earth again and again with the pure and perennial waters of spiritual truth. Hence have proceeded the tidal waves of philosophy that have covered the earth, East or West, North or South, and hence again must start the wave which is going to spiritualise the material civilisation of the world. Here is the life-giving water with which must be quenched the burning fire of materialism which is burning the core of the hearts of millions in other lands. Believe me, my friends, this is going to be.

So much I have seen, and so far those of you who are students of the history of races are already aware of this fact. The debt which the world owes to our Motherland is immense. Taking country with country, there is not one race on this earth to which the world owes so much as to the patient Hindu, the mild Hindu. "The mild Hindu" sometimes is used as an expression of reproach; but if ever a reproach concealed a wonderful truth, it is in the term, "the mild Hindu", who has always been the blessed child of God. Civilisations have arisen in other parts of the world. In ancient times and in modern times, great ideas have emanated from strong and great races. In ancient and in modern times, wonderful ideas have been carried forward from one race to another. In ancient and in modern times, seeds of great truth and power have been cast abroad by the advancing tides of national life; but mark you, my friends, it has been always with the blast of war trumpets and with the march of embattled cohorts. Each idea had to be soaked in a deluge of blood. Each idea had to wade through the blood of millions of our fellow-beings. Each word of power had to be followed by the groans of millions, by the wails of orphans, by the tears of widows. This, in the main, other nations have taught; but India has for thousands of years peacefully existed. Here activity prevailed when even Greece did not exist, when Rome was not thought of, when the very fathers of the modern Europeans lived in the forests and painted themselves blue. Even earlier, when history has no record, and tradition dares not peer into the gloom of that intense past, even from then until now, ideas after ideas have marched out from her, but every word has been spoken with a blessing behind it and peace before it. We, of all nations of the world, have never been a conquering race, and that blessing is on our head, and therefore we live.

There was a time when at the sound of the march of big Greek battalions the earth trembled. Vanished from off the face of the earth, with not every a tale left behind to tell, gone is that ancient land of the Greeks. There was a time when the Roman Eagle floated over everything worth having in this world; everywhere Rome's power was felt and pressed on the head of humanity; the earth trembled at the name of Rome. But the Capitoline Hill is a mass of ruins, the spider weaves its web where the Caesars ruled. There have been other nations equally glorious that have come and gone, living a few hours of exultant and exuberant dominance and of a wicked national life, and then vanishing like ripples on the face of the waters. Thus have these nations made their mark on the face of humanity. But we live, and if Manu came back today he would not be bewildered, and would not find himself in a foreign land. The same laws are here, laws adjusted and thought out through thousands and thousands of years; customs, the outcome of the acumen of ages and the experience of centuries, that seem to be eternal; and as the days go by, as blow after blow of misfortune has been delivered upon them, such blows seem to have served one purpose only, that of making them stronger and more constant. And to find the centre of all this, the heart from which the blood flows, the mainspring of the national life, believe me when I say after my experience of the world, that it is here.

To the other nations of the world, religion is one among the many occupations of life. There is politics, there are the enjoyments of social life, there is all that wealth can buy or power can bring, there is all that the senses can enjoy; and among all these various occupations of life and all this searching after something which can give yet a little more whetting to the cloyed senses — among all these, there is perhaps a little bit of religion. But here, in India, religion is the one and the only occupation of life. How many of you know that there has been a Sino-Japanese War? Very few of you, if any. That there are tremendous political movements and socialistic movements trying to transform Western society, how many of you know? Very few indeed, if any. But that there was a Parliament of Religions in America, and that there was a Hindu Sannyâsin sent over there, I am astonished to find that even the cooly knows of it. That shows the way the wind blows, where the national life is. I used to read books written by globe-trotting travellers, especially foreigners, who deplored the ignorance of the Eastern masses, but I found out that it was partly true and at the same time partly untrue. If you ask a ploughman in England, or America, or France, or Germany to what party he belongs, he can tell you whether he belongs to the Radicals or the Conservatives, and for whom he is going to vote. In America he will say whether he is Republican or Democrat, and he even knows something about the silver question. But if you ask him about his religion, he will tell you that he goes to church and belongs to a certain denomination. That is all he knows, and he thinks it is sufficient.

Now, when we come to India, if you ask one of our ploughmen, "Do you know anything about politics?" He will reply, "What is that?" He does not understand the socialistic movements, the relation between capital and labour, and all that; he has never heard of such things in his life, he works hard and earns his bread. But you ask, "What is your religion?" he replies, "Look here, my friend, I have marked it on my forehead." He can give you a good hint or two on questions of religion. That has been my experience. That is our nation's life.

Individuals have each their own peculiarities, and each man has his own method of growth, his own life marked out for him by the infinite past life, by all his past Karma as we Hindus say. Into this world he comes with all the past on him, the infinite past ushèrs the present, and the way in which we use the present is going to make the future. Thus everyone born into this world has a bent, a direction towards which he must go, through which he must live, and what is true of the individual is equally true of the race. Each race, similarly, has a peculiar bent, each race has a peculiar raison d'être , each race has a peculiar mission to fulfil in the life of the world. Each race has to make its own result, to fulfil its own mission. Political greatness or military power is never the mission of our race; it never was, and, mark my words, it never will be. But there has been the other mission given to us, which is to conserve, to preserve, to accumulate, as it were, into a dynamo, all the spiritual energy of the race, and that concentrated energy is to pour forth in a deluge on the world whenever circumstances are propitious. Let the Persian or the Greek, the Roman, the Arab, or the Englishman march his battalions, conquer the world, and link the different nations together, and the philosophy and spirituality of India is ever ready to flow along the new-made channels into the veins of the nations of the world. The Hindu's calm brain must pour out its own quota to give to the sum total of human progress. India's gift to the world is the light spiritual.

Thus, in the past, we read in history that whenever there arose a greet conquering nation uniting the different races of the world, binding India with the other races, taking her out, as it were, from her loneliness and from her aloofness from the rest of the world into which she again and again cast herself, that whenever such a state has been brought about, the result has been the flooding of the world with Indian spiritual ideas. At the beginning of this century, Schopenhauer, the great German philosopher, studying from a not very clear translation of the Vedas made from an old translation into Persian and thence by a young Frenchman into Latin, says, "In the whole world there is no study so beneficial and so elevating as that of the Upanishads. It has been the solace of my life, it will be the solace of my death." This great German sage foretold that "The world is about to see a revolution in thought more extensive and more powerful than that which was witnessed by the Renaissance of Greek Literature", and today his predictions are coming to pass. Those who keep their eyes open, those who understand the workings in the minds of different nations of the West, those who are thinkers and study the different nations, will find the immense change that has been produced in the tone, the procedure, in the methods, and in the literature of the world by this slow, never-ceasing permeation of Indian thought.

But there is another peculiarity, as I have already hinted to you. We never preached our thoughts with fire and sword. If there is one word in the English language to represent the gift of India to the world, if there is one word in the English language to express the effect which the literature of India produces upon mankind, it is this one word, "fascination". It is the opposite of anything that takes you suddenly; it throws on you, as it were, a charm imperceptibly. To many, Indian thought, Indian manners; Indian customs, Indian philosophy, Indian literature are repulsive at the first sight; but let them persevere, let them read, let them become familiar with the great principles underlying these ideas, and it is ninety-nine to one that the charm will come over them, and fascination will be the result. Slow and silent, as the gentle dew that falls in the morning, unseen and unheard yet producing a most tremendous result, has been the work of the calm, patient, all-suffering spiritual race upon the world of thought.

Once more history is going to repeat itself. For today, under the blasting light of modern science, when old and apparently strong and invulnerable beliefs have been shattered to their very foundations, when special claims laid to the allegiance of mankind by different sects have been all blown into atoms and have vanished into air, when the sledge-hammer blows of modern antiquarian researches are pulverising like masses of porcelain all sorts of antiquated orthodoxies, when religion in the West is only in the hands of the ignorant and the knowing ones look down with scorn upon anything belonging to religion, here comes to the fore the philosophy of India, which displays the highest religious aspirations of the Indian mind, where the grandest philosophical facts have been the practical spirituality of the people. This naturally

is coming to the rescue, the idea of the oneness of all, the Infinite, the idea of the Impersonal, the wonderful idea of the eternal soul of man, of the unbroken continuity in the march of beings, and the infinity of the universe. The old sects looked upon the world as a little mud-puddle and thought that time began but the other day. It was there in our old books, and only there that the grand idea of the infinite range of time, space, and causation, and above all, the infinite glory of the spirit of man governed all the search for religion. When the modern tremendous theories of evolution and conservation of energy and so forth are dealing death blows to all sorts of crude theologies, what can hold any more the allegiance of cultured humanity but the most wonderful, convincing, broadening, and ennobling ideas that can be found only in that most marvellous product of the soul of man, the wonderful voice of God, the Vedanta?

At the same time, I must remark that what I mean by our religion working upon the nations outside of India comprises only the principles, the background, the foundation upon which that religion is built. The detailed workings, the minute points which have been worked out through centuries of social necessity, little ratiocinations about manners and customs and social well-being, do not rightly find a place in the category of religion. We know that in our books a clear distinction is made between two sets of truths. The one set is that which abides for ever, being built upon the nature of man, the nature of the soul, the soul's relation to God, the nature of God, perfection, and so on; there are also the principles of cosmology, of the infinitude of creation, or more correctly speaking — projection, the wonderful law of cyclical procession, and so on — these are the eternal principles founded upon the universal laws in nature. The other set comprises the minor laws which guided the working of our everyday life They belong more properly to the Purânas, to the Smritis, and not to the Shrutis. These have nothing to do with the other principles. Even in our own nation these minor laws have been changing all the time. Customs of one age, of one Yuga, have not been the customs of another, and as Yuga comes after Yuga, they will still have to change. Great Rishis will appear and lead us to customs and manners that are suited to new environments.

The great principles underlying all this wonderful, infinite, ennobling, expansive view of man and God and the world have been produced in India. In India alone man has not stood up to fight for a little tribal God, saying "My God is true and yours is not true; let us have a good fight over it." It was only here that such ideas did not occur as fighting for little gods. These great underlying principles, being based upon the eternal nature of man, are as potent today for working for the good of the human race as they were thousands of years ago, and they will remain so, so long as this earth remains, so long as the law of Karma remains, so long as we are born as individuals and have to work out our own destiny by our individual power.

And above all, what India has to give to the world is this. If we watch the growth and development of religions in different races, we shall always find this that each tribe at the beginning has a god of its own. If the tribes are allied to each other, these gods will have a generic name, as for example, all the Babylonian gods had. When the Babylonians were divided into many races, they had the generic name of Baal, just as the Jewish races had different gods with the common name of Moloch; and at the same time you will find that one of these tribes becomes superior to the rest, and lays claim to its own king as the king over all. Therefrom it naturally follows that it also wants to preserve its own god as the god of all the races. Baal-Merodach, said the Babylonians, was the greatest god; all the others were inferior. Moloch-Yahveh was the superior over all other Molochs. And these questions had to be decided by the fortunes of battle. The same struggle was here also. In India the same competing gods had been struggling with each other for supremacy, but the great good fortune of this country and of the world was that there came out in the midst of the din and confusion a voice which declared — "That which exists is One; sages call It by various names." It is not that Shiva is superior to Vishnu, not that Vishnu is everything and Shiva is nothing, but it is the same one whom you call either Shiva, or Vishnu, or by a hundred other names. The names are different, but it is the same one. The whole history of India you may read in these few words. The whole history has been a repetition in massive language, with tremendous power, of that one central doctrine. It was repeated in the land till it had entered into the blood of the nation, till it began to tingle with every drop of blood that flowed in its veins, till it became one with the life, part and parcel of the material of which it was composed; and thus the land was transmuted into the most wonderful land of toleration, giving the right to welcome the various religions as well as all sects into the old mother-country.

And herein is the explanation of the most remarkable phenomenon that is only witnessed here — all the various sects, apparently hopelessly contradictory, yet living in such harmony. You may be a dualist, and I may be a monist. You may believe that you are the eternal servant of God, and I may declare that I am one with

God Himself; yet both of us are good Hindus. How is that possible? Read then — "That which exists is One; sages call It by various names." Above all others, my countrymen, this is the one grand truth that we have to teach to the world. Even the most educated people of other countries turn up their noses at an angle of forty-five degrees and call our religion idolatry. I have seen that; and they never stopped to think what a mass of superstition there was in their own heads. It is still so everywhere, this tremendous sectarianism, the low narrowness of the mind. The thing which a man has is the only thing worth having; the only life worth living is his own little life of dollar-worship and mammon-worship; the only little possession worth having is his own property, and nothing else. If he can manufacture a little clay nonsense or invent a machine, that is to be admired beyond the greatest possessions. That is the case over the whole world in spite of education and learning. But education has yet to be in the world, and civilisation — civilisation has begun nowhere yet. Ninety-nine decimal nine per cent of the human race are more or less savages even now. We may read of these things in books, and we hear of toleration in religion and all that, but very little of it is there yet in the world; take my experience for that. Ninety-nine per cent do not even think of it. There is tremendous religious persecution yet in every country in which I have been, and the same old objections are raised against learning anything new. The little toleration that is in the world, the little sympathy that is yet in the world for religious thought, is practically here in the land of the Aryan, and nowhere else. It is here that Indians build temples for Mohammedans and Christians; nowhere else. If you go to other countries and ask Mohammedans or people of other religions to build a temple for you, see how they will help. They will instead try to break down your temple and you too if they can. The one great lesson, therefore, that the world wants most, that the world has yet to learn from India, is the idea not only of toleration, but of sympathy. Well has it been said in the Mahimnah-stotra : "As the different rivers, taking their start from different mountains, running straight or crooked, at last come unto the ocean, so, O Shiva, the different paths which men take through different tendencies, various though they appear, crooked or straight, all lead unto These." Though they may take various roads, all are on the ways. Some may run a little crooked, others may run straight, but at last they will all come unto the Lord, the One. Then and then alone, is your Bhakti of Shiva complete when you not only see Him in the Linga, but you see Him everywhere. He is the sage, he is the lover of Hari who sees Hari in everything and in everyone. If you are a real lover of Shiva, you must see Him in everything and in everyone. You must see that every worship is given unto Him whatever may be the name or the form; that all knees bending towards the Caaba, or kneeling in a Christian church, or in a Buddhist temple are kneeling to Him whether they know it or not, whether they are conscious of it or not; that in whatever name or form they are offered, all these flowers are laid at His feet; for He is the one Lord of all, the one Soul of all souls. He knows infinitely better what this world wants than you or I. It is impossible that all difference can cease; it must exist; without variation life must cease. It is this clash, the differentiation of thought that makes for light, for motion, for everything. Differentiation, infinitely contradictory, must remain, but it is not necessary that we should hate each other therefore; it is not necessary therefore that we should fight each other.

Therefore we have again to learn the one central truth that was preached only here in our Motherland, and that has to be preached once more from India. Why? Because not only is it in our books, but it runs through every phase of our national literature and is in the national life. Here and here alone is it practiced every day, and any man whose eyes are open can see that it is practiced here and here alone. Thus we have to teach religion. There are other and higher lessons that India can teach, but they are only for the learned. The lessons of mildness, gentleness, forbearance, toleration, sympathy, and brotherhood, everyone may learn, whether man, woman, or child, learned or unlearned, without respect of race, caste, or creed. "They call Thee by various names; Thou art One."

Addresses At the Parliament of Religions

Response To Welcome

At the World's Parliament of Religions, Chicago 11th September, 1893

Sisters and Brothers of America,

It fills my heart with joy unspeakable to rise in response to the warm and cordial welcome which you have given us. I thank you in the name of the most ancient order of monks in the world; I thank you in the name of the mother of religions; and I thank you in the name of millions and millions of Hindu people of all classes and sects.

My thanks, also, to some of the speakers on this platform who, referring to the delegates from the Orient, have told you that these men from far-off nations may well claim the honour of bearing to different lands the idea of toleration. I am proud to belong to a religion which has taught the world both tolerance and universal acceptance. We believe not only in universal toleration, but we accept all religions as true. I am proud to belong to a nation which has sheltered the persecuted and the refugees of all religions and all nations of the earth. I am proud to tell you that we have gathered in our bosom the purest remnant of the Israelites, who came to Southern India and took refuge with us in the very year in which their holy temple was shattered to pieces by Roman tyranny. I am proud to belong to the religion which has sheltered and is still fostering the remnant of the grand Zoroastrian nation. I will quote to you, brethren, a few lines from a hymn which I remember to have repeated from my earliest boyhood, which is every day repeated by millions of human beings: "As the different streams having their sources in different places all mingle their water in the sea, so, O Lord, the different paths which men take through different tendencies, various though they appear, crooked or straight, all lead to Thee ."

The present convention, which is one of the most august assemblies ever held, is in itself a vindication, a declaration to the world of the wonderful doctrine preached in the Gita: "Whosoever comes to Me, through whatsoever form, I reach him; all men are struggling through paths which in the end lead to me ." Sectarianism, bigotry, and its horrible descendant, fanaticism, have long possessed this beautiful earth. They have filled the earth with violence, drenched it often and often with human blood, destroyed civilisation and sent whole nations to despair. Had it not been for these horrible demons, human society would be far more advanced than it is now. But their time is come; and I fervently hope that the bell that tolled this morning in honour of this convention may be the death-knell of all fanaticism, of all persecutions with the sword or with the pen, and of all uncharitable feelings between persons wending their way to the same goal.

Why We Disagree

15th September, 1893

I will tell you a little story. You have heard the eloquent speaker who has just finished say, "Let us cease from abusing each other," and he was very sorry that there should be always so much variance.

But I think I should tell you a story which would illustrate the cause of this variance. A frog lived in a well. It had lived there for a long time. It was born there and brought up there, and yet was a little, small frog. Of course the evolutionists were not there then to tell us whether the frog lost its eyes or not, but, for our story's sake, we must take it for granted that it had its eyes, and that it every day cleansed the water of all the worms and bacilli that lived in it with an energy that would do credit to our modern bacteriologists. In this way it went on and became a little sleek and fat. Well, one day another frog that lived in the sea came and fell into the well.

"Where are you from?"

"I am from the sea."

"The sea! How big is that? Is it as big as my well?" and he took a leap from one side of the well to the other.

"My friend," said the frog of the sea, "how do you compare the sea with your little well?"

Then the frog took another leap and asked, "Is your sea so big?"

"What nonsense you speak, to compare the sea with your well!"

"Well, then," said the frog of the well, "nothing can be bigger than my well; there can be nothing bigger than this; this fellow is a liar, so turn him out."

That has been the difficulty all the while.

I am a Hindu. I am sitting in my own little well and thinking that the whole world is my little well. The Christian sits in his little well and thinks the whole world is his well. The Mohammedan sits in his little well and thinks that is the whole world. I have to thank you of America for the great attempt you are making to break down the barriers of this little world of ours, and hope that, in the future, the Lord will help you to accomplish your purpose.

Paper On Hinduism

Read at the Parliament on 19th September, 1893

Three religions now stand in the world which have come down to us from time prehistoric — Hinduism, Zoroastrianism and Judaism. They have all received tremendous shocks and all of them prove by their survival their internal strength. But while Judaism failed to absorb Christianity and was driven out of its place of birth by its all-conquering daughter, and a handful of Parsees is all that remains to tell the tale of their grand religion, sect after sect arose in India and seemed to shake the religion of the Vedas to its very foundations, but like the waters of the seashore in a tremendous earthquake it receded only for a while, only to return in an all-absorbing flood, a thousand times more vigorous, and when the tumult of the rush was over, these sects were all sucked in, absorbed, and assimilated into the immense body of the mother faith.

From the high spiritual flights of the Vedanta philosophy, of which the latest discoveries of science seem like echoes, to the low ideas of idolatry with its multifarious mythology, the agnosticism of the Buddhists, and the atheism of the Jains, each and all have a place in the Hindu's religion.

Where then, the question arises, where is the common centre to which all these widely diverging radii converge? Where is the common basis upon which all these seemingly hopeless contradictions rest? And this is the question I shall attempt to answer.

The Hindus have received their religion through revelation, the Vedas. They hold that the Vedas are without beginning and without end. It may sound ludicrous to this audience, how a book can be without beginning or end. But by the Vedas no books are meant. They mean the accumulated treasury of spiritual laws discovered by different persons in different times. Just as the law of gravitation existed before its discovery, and would exist if all humanity forgot it, so is it with the laws that govern the spiritual world. The moral, ethical, and spiritual relations between soul and soul and between individual spirits and the Father of all spirits, were there before their discovery, and would remain even if we forgot them.

The discoverers of these laws are called Rishis, and we honour them as perfected beings. I am glad to tell this audience that some of the very greatest of them were women. Here it may be said that these laws as laws may be without end, but they must have had a beginning. The Vedas teach us that creation is without beginning or end. Science is said to have proved that the sum total of cosmic energy is always the same. Then, if there was a time when nothing existed, where was all this manifested energy? Some say it was in a potential form in God. In that case God is sometimes potential and sometimes kinetic, which would make Him mutable. Everything mutable is a compound, and everything compound must undergo that change which is called destruction. So God would die, which is absurd. Therefore there never was a time when there was no creation.

If I may be allowed to use a simile, creation and creator are two lines, without beginning and without end, running parallel to each other. God is the ever active providence, by whose power systems after systems are being evolved out of chaos, made to run for a time and again destroyed. This is what the Brâhmin boy repeats every day: “The sun and the moon, the Lord created like the suns and moons of previous cycles .” And this agrees with modern science.

Here I stand and if I shut my eyes, and try to conceive my existence, "I", "I", "I", what is the idea before me? The idea of a body. Am I, then, nothing but a combination of material substances? The Vedas declare, "No". I am a spirit living in a body. I am not the body. The body will die, but I shall not die. Here am I in this body; it will fall, but I shall go on living. I had also a past. The soul was not created, for creation means a combination which means a certain future dissolution. If then the soul was created, it must die. Some are born happy, enjoy perfect health, with beautiful body, mental vigour and all wants supplied. Others are born miserable, some are without hands or feet, others again are idiots and only drag on a wretched existence. Why, if they are all created, why does a just and merciful God create one happy and another unhappy, why is He so partial? Nor would it mend matters in the least to hold that those who are miserable in this life will be happy in a future one. Why should a man be miserable even here in the reign of a just and merciful God?

In the second place, the idea of a creator God does not explain the anomaly, but simply expresses the cruel fiat of an all-powerful being. There must have been causes, then, before his birth, to make a man miserable or happy and those were his past actions.

Are not all the tendencies of the mind and the body accounted for by inherited aptitude? Here are two parallel lines of existence — one of the mind, the other of matter. If matter and its transformations answer for all that we have, there is no necessity for supposing the existence of a soul. But it cannot be proved that thought has been evolved out of matter, and if a philosophical monism is inevitable, spiritual monism is certainly logical and no less desirable than a materialistic monism; but neither of these is necessary here.

We cannot deny that bodies acquire certain tendencies from heredity, but those tendencies only mean the physical configuration, through which a peculiar mind alone can act in a peculiar way. There are other tendencies peculiar to a soul caused by its past actions. And a soul with a certain tendency would by the laws of affinity take birth in a body which is the fittest instrument for the display of that tendency. This is in accord with science, for science wants to explain everything by habit, and habit is got through repetitions. So repetitions are necessary to explain the natural habits of a new-born soul. And since they were not obtained in this present life, they must have come down from past lives.

There is another suggestion. Taking all these for granted, how is it that I do not remember anything of my past life ? This can be easily explained. I am now speaking English. It is not my mother tongue, in fact no words of my mother tongue are now present in my consciousness; but let me try to bring them up, and they rush in. That shows that consciousness is only the surface of the mental ocean, and within its depths are stored up all our experiences. Try and struggle, they would come up and you would be conscious even of your past life.

This is direct and demonstrative evidence. Verification is the perfect proof of a theory, and here is the challenge thrown to the world by the Rishis. We have discovered the secret by which the very depths of the ocean of memory can be stirred up — try it and you would get a complete reminiscence of your past life.

So then the Hindu believes that he is a spirit. Him the sword cannot pierce — him the fire cannot burn — him the water cannot melt — him the air cannot dry. The Hindu believes that every soul is a circle whose circumference is nowhere, but whose centre is located in the body, and that death means the change of this centre from body to body. Nor is the soul bound by the conditions of matter. In its very essence it is free, unbounded, holy, pure, and perfect. But somehow or other it finds itself tied down to matter, and thinks of itself as matter.

Why should the free, perfect, and pure being be thus under the thraldom of matter, is the next question. How can the perfect soul be deluded into the belief that it is imperfect? We have been told that the Hindus shirk the question and say that no such question can be there. Some thinkers want to answer it by positing one or more quasi-perfect beings, and use big scientific names to fill up the gap. But naming is not explaining. The question remains the same. How can the perfect become the quasi-perfect; how can the pure, the absolute, change even a microscopic particle of its nature? But the Hindu is sincere. He does not want to take shelter under sophistry. He is brave enough to face the question in a manly fashion; and his answer is: " I do not know. I do not know how the perfect being, the soul, came to think of itself as imperfect, as joined to and conditioned by matter." But the fact is a fact for all that. It is a fact in everybody's consciousness that one thinks of oneself as the body. The Hindu does not attempt to explain why one thinks one is the body. The answer that it is the will of God is no explanation. This is nothing more than what the Hindu says, "I do not know."

Well, then, the human soul is eternal and immortal, perfect and infinite, and death means only a change of centre from one body to another. The present is determined by our past actions, and the future by the present. The soul will go on evolving up or reverting back from birth to birth and death to death. But here is another question: Is man a tiny boat in a tempest, raised one moment on the foamy crest of a billow and dashed down into a yawning chasm the next, rolling to and fro at the mercy of good and bad actions — a powerless, helpless wreck in an ever-raging, ever-rushing, uncompromising current of cause and effect; a little moth placed under the wheel of causation which rolls on crushing everything in its way and waits not for the widow's tears or the orphan's cry? The heart sinks at the idea, yet this is the law of Nature. Is there no hope? Is there no escape? — was the cry that went up from the bottom of the heart of despair. It reached the throne of mercy, and words of hope and consolation came down and inspired a Vedic sage, and he stood up before the world and in trumpet voice proclaimed the glad tidings: "Hear, ye children of immortal bliss! even ye that reside in higher spheres! I have found the Ancient One who is beyond all darkness, all delusion: knowing Him alone you shall be saved from death over again." "Children of immortal bliss" — what a sweet, what a hopeful name! Allow me to call you, brethren, by that sweet name — heirs of immortal bliss — yea, the Hindu refuses to call you sinners. Ye are the Children of God, the sharers of immortal bliss, holy and perfect beings. Ye divinities on earth — sinners! It is a sin to call a man so; it is a standing libel on human nature. Come up, O lions, and shake off the delusion that you are sheep; you are souls immortal, spirits free, blest and eternal; ye are not matter, ye are not bodies; matter is your servant, not you the servant of matter.

Thus it is that the Vedas proclaim not a dreadful combination of unforgiving laws, not an endless prison of cause and effect, but that at the head of all these laws, in and through every particle of matter and force, stands One "by whose command the wind blows, the fire burns, the clouds rain, and death stalks upon the earth."

And what is His nature?

He is everywhere, the pure and formless One, the Almighty and the All-merciful. "Thou art our father, Thou art our mother, Thou art our beloved friend, Thou art the source of all strength; give us strength. Thou art He that beareth the burdens of the universe; help me bear the little burden of this life." Thus sang the Rishis of the Vedas. And how to worship Him? Through love. "He is to be worshipped as the one beloved, dearer than everything in this and the next life."

This is the doctrine of love declared in the Vedas, and let us see how it is fully developed and taught by Krishna, whom the Hindus believe to have been God incarnate on earth.

He taught that a man ought to live in this world like a lotus leaf, which grows in water but is never moistened by water; so a man ought to live in the world — his heart to God and his hands to work.

It is good to love God for hope of reward in this or the next world, but it is better to love God for love's sake, and the prayer goes: "Lord, I do not want wealth, nor children, nor learning. If it be Thy will, I shall go from birth to birth, but grant me this, that I may love Thee without the hope of reward — love unselfishly for love's sake." One of the disciples of Krishna, the then Emperor of India, was driven from his kingdom by his enemies and had to take shelter with his queen in a forest in the Himalayas, and there one day the queen asked him how it was that he, the most virtuous of men, should suffer so much misery. Yudhishthira answered, "Behold, my queen, the Himalayas, how grand and beautiful they are; I love them. They do not give me anything, but my nature is to love the grand, the beautiful, therefore I love them. Similarly, I love the Lord. He is the source of all beauty, of all sublimity. He is the only object to be loved; my nature is to love Him, and therefore I love. I do not pray for anything; I do not ask for anything. Let Him place me wherever He likes. I must love Him for love's sake. I cannot trade in love."

The Vedas teach that the soul is divine, only held in the bondage of matter; perfection will be reached when this bond will burst, and the word they use for it is therefore, Mukti — freedom, freedom from the bonds of imperfection, freedom from death and misery.

And this bondage can only fall off through the mercy of God, and this mercy comes on the pure. So purity is the condition of His mercy. How does that mercy act? He reveals Himself to the pure heart; the pure and the stainless see God, yea, even in this life; then and then only all the crookedness of the heart is made straight. Then all doubt ceases. He is no more the freak of a terrible law of causation. This is the very centre, the very vital conception of Hinduism. The Hindu does not want to live upon words and theories. If there are existences beyond the ordinary sensuous existence, he wants to come face to face with them. If there is a soul in him which is not matter, if there is an all-merciful universal Soul, he will go to Him direct. He must see Him, and that alone can destroy all doubts. So the best proof a Hindu sage gives about the soul, about God, is: "I have seen the soul; I have seen God." And that is the only condition of perfection. The Hindu religion does not consist in struggles and attempts to believe a certain doctrine or dogma, but in realising — not in believing, but in being and becoming.

Thus the whole object of their system is by constant struggle to become perfect, to become divine, to reach God and see God, and this reaching God, seeing God, becoming perfect even as the Father in Heaven is perfect, constitutes the religion of the Hindus.

And what becomes of a man when he attains perfection? He lives a life of bliss infinite. He enjoys infinite and perfect bliss, having obtained the only thing in which man ought to have pleasure, namely God, and enjoys the bliss with God.

So far all the Hindus are agreed. This is the common religion of all the sects of India; but, then, perfection is absolute, and the absolute cannot be two or three. It cannot have any qualities. It cannot be an individual. And so when a soul becomes perfect and absolute, it must become one with Brahman, and it would only realise the Lord as the perfection, the reality, of its own nature and existence, the existence absolute, knowledge absolute, and bliss absolute. We have often and often read this called the losing of individuality and becoming a stock or a stone.

"He jests at scars that never felt a wound."

I tell you it is nothing of the kind. If it is happiness to enjoy the consciousness of this small body, it must be greater happiness to enjoy the consciousness of two bodies, the measure of happiness increasing with the consciousness of an increasing number of bodies, the aim, the ultimate of happiness being reached when it would become a universal consciousness.

Therefore, to gain this infinite universal individuality, this miserable little prison-individuality must go. Then alone can death cease when I am alone with life, then alone can misery cease when I am one with happiness itself, then alone can all errors cease when I am one with knowledge itself; and this is the necessary scientific conclusion. Science has proved to me that physical individuality is a delusion, that really my body is one little continuously changing body in an unbroken ocean of matter; and Advaita (unity) is the necessary conclusion with my other counterpart, soul.

Science is nothing but the finding of unity. As soon as science would reach perfect unity, it would stop from further progress, because it would reach the goal. Thus Chemistry could not progress farther when it would discover one element out of which all other could be made. Physics would stop when it would be able to fulfill its services in discovering one energy of which all others are but manifestations, and the science of religion become perfect when it would discover Him who is the one life in a universe of death, Him who is the constant basis of an ever-changing world. One who is the only Soul of which all souls are but delusive manifestations. Thus is it, through multiplicity and duality, that the ultimate unity is reached. Religion can go no farther. This is the goal of all science.

All science is bound to come to this conclusion in the long run. Manifestation, and not creation, is the word of science today, and the Hindu is only glad that what he has been cherishing in his bosom for ages is going to be taught in more forcible language, and with further light from the latest conclusions of science.

Descend we now from the aspirations of philosophy to the religion of the ignorant. At the very outset, I may tell you that there is no polytheism in India. In every temple, if one stands by and listens, one will find the worshippers applying all the attributes of God, including omnipresence, to the images. It is not polytheism, nor would the name henotheism explain the situation. "The rose called by any other name would smell as sweet." Names are not explanations.

I remember, as a boy, hearing a Christian missionary preach to a crowd in India. Among other sweet things he was telling them was that if he gave a blow to their idol with his stick, what could it do? One of his hearers sharply answered, "If I abuse your God, what can He do?" "You would be punished," said the preacher, "when you die." "So my idol will punish you when you die," retorted the Hindu.

The tree is known by its fruits. When I have seen amongst them that are called idolaters, men, the like of whom in morality and spirituality and love I have never seen anywhere, I stop and ask myself, “Can sin beget holiness?”

Superstition is a great enemy of man, but bigotry is worse. Why does a Christian go to church? Why is the cross holy? Why is the face turned toward the sky in prayer? Why are there so many images in the Catholic Church? Why are there so many images in the minds of Protestants when they pray? My brethren, we can no more think about anything without a mental image than we can live without breathing. By the law of association, the material image calls up the mental idea and vice versa . This is why the Hindu uses an external symbol when he worships. He will tell you, it helps to keep his mind fixed on the Being to whom he prays. He knows as well as you do that the image is not God, is not omnipresent. After all, how much does omnipresence mean to almost the whole world? It stands merely as a word, a symbol. Has God superficial area? If not, when we repeat that word “omnipresent”, we think of the extended sky or of space, that is all.

As we find that somehow or other, by the laws of our mental constitution, we have to associate our ideas of infinity with the image of the blue sky, or of the sea, so we naturally connect our idea of holiness with the image of a church, a mosque, or a cross. The Hindus have associated the idea of holiness, purity, truth, omnipresence, and such other ideas with different images and forms. But with this difference that while some people devote their whole lives to their idol of a church and never rise higher, because with them religion means an intellectual assent to certain doctrines and doing good to their fellows, the whole religion of the Hindu is centred in realisation. Man is to become divine by realising the divine. Idols or temples or churches or books are only the supports, the helps, of his spiritual childhood: but on and on he must progress.

He must not stop anywhere. "External worship, material worship, " say the scriptures, "is the lowest stage; struggling to rise high, mental prayer is the next stage, but the highest stage is when the Lord has been realised ." Mark, the same earnest man who is kneeling before the idol tells you, "Him the Sun cannot express, nor the moon, nor the stars, the lightning cannot express Him, nor what we speak of as fire; through Him they shine ." But he does not abuse any one's idol or call its worship sin. He recognises in it a necessary stage of life. "The child is father of the man ." Would it be right for an old man to say that childhood is a sin or youth a sin?

If a man can realise his divine nature with the help of an image, would it be right to call that a sin? Nor even when he has passed that stage, should he call it an error. To the Hindu, man is not travelling from error to truth, but from truth to truth, from lower to higher truth. To him all the religions, from the lowest fetishism to the highest absolutism, mean so many attempts of the human soul to grasp and realise the Infinite, each determined by the conditions of its birth and association, and each of these marks a stage of progress; and every soul is a young eagle soaring higher and higher, gathering more and more strength, till it reaches the Glorious Sun.

Unity in variety is the plan of nature, and the Hindu has recognised it. Every other religion lays down certain fixed dogmas, and tries to force society to adopt them. It places before society only one coat which must fit Jack and John and Henry, all alike. If it does not fit John or Henry, he must go without a coat to cover his body. The Hindus have discovered that the absolute can only be realised, or thought of, or stated, through the relative, and the images, crosses, and crescents are simply so many symbols — so many pegs to hang the spiritual ideas on. It is not that this help is necessary for every one, but those that do not need it have no right to say that it is wrong. Nor is it compulsory in Hinduism.

One thing I must tell you. Idolatry in India does not mean anything horrible. It is not the mother of harlots. On the other hand, it is the attempt of undeveloped minds to grasp high spiritual truths. The Hindus have their faults, they sometimes have their exceptions; but mark this, they are always for punishing their own bodies, and never for cutting the throats of their neighbours. If the Hindu fanatic burns himself on the pyre, he never lights the fire of Inquisition. And even this cannot be laid at the door of his religion any more than the burning of witches can be laid at the door of Christianity.

To the Hindu, then, the whole world of religions is only a travelling, a coming up, of different men and women, through various conditions and circumstances, to the same goal. Every religion is only evolving a God out of the material man, and the same God is the inspirer of all of them. Why, then, are there so many contradictions? They are only apparent, says the Hindu. The contradictions come from the same truth adapting itself to the varying circumstances of different natures.

It is the same light coming through glasses of different colours. And these little variations are necessary for purposes of adaptation. But in the heart of everything the same truth reigns. The Lord has declared to the Hindu in His incarnation as Krishna, "I am in every religion as the thread through a string of pearls. Wherever thou seest extraordinary holiness and extraordinary power raising and purifying humanity, know thou that I am there ." And what has been the result? I challenge the world to find, throughout the whole system of Sanskrit philosophy, any such expression as that the Hindu alone will be saved and not others. Says Vyasa, "We find perfect men even beyond the pale of our caste and creed ." One thing more. How, then, can the Hindu, whose whole fabric of thought centres in God, believe in Buddhism which is agnostic, or in Jainism which is atheistic?

The Buddhists or the Jains do not depend upon God; but the whole force of their religion is directed to the great central truth in every religion, to evolve a God out of man. They have not seen the Father, but they have seen the Son. And he that hath seen the Son hath seen the Father also.

This, brethren, is a short sketch of the religious ideas of the Hindus. The Hindu may have failed to carry out all his plans, but if there is ever to be a universal religion, it must be one which will have no location in place or time; which will be infinite like the God it will preach, and whose sun will shine upon the followers of Krishna and of Christ, on saints and sinners alike; which will not be Brahminic or Buddhistic, Christian or Mohammedan, but the sum total of all these, and still have infinite space for development; which in its catholicity will embrace in its infinite arms, and find a place for, every human being, from the lowest grovelling savage not far removed from the brute, to the highest man towering by the virtues of his head and heart almost above humanity, making society stand in awe of him and doubt his human nature. It will be a religion which will have no place for persecution or intolerance in its polity, which will recognise divinity in every man and woman, and whose whole scope, whose whole force, will be created in aiding humanity to realise its own true, divine nature.

Offer such a religion, and all the nations will follow you. Asoka's council was a council of the Buddhist faith. Akbar's, though more to the purpose, was only a parlour-meeting. It was reserved for America to proclaim to all quarters of the globe that the Lord is in every religion.

May He who is the Brahman of the Hindus, the Ahura-Mazda of the Zoroastrians, the Buddha of the Buddhists, the Jehovah of the Jews, the Father in Heaven of the Christians, give strength to you to carry out your noble idea! The star arose in the East; it travelled steadily towards the West, sometimes dimmed and sometimes effulgent, till it made a circuit of the world; and now it is again rising on the very horizon of the East, the borders of the Sanpo, a thousandfold more effulgent than it ever was before.

Hail, Columbia, motherland of liberty! It has been given to thee, who never dipped her hand in her neighbour's blood, who never found out that the shortest way of becoming rich was by robbing one's neighbours, it has been given to thee to march at the vanguard of civilisation with the flag of harmony.

Religion Not the Crying Need of India

20th September, 1893

Christians must always be ready for good criticism, and I hardly think that you will mind if I make a little criticism. You Christians, who are so fond of sending out missionaries to save the soul of the heathen — why do you not try to save their bodies from starvation? In India, during the terrible famines, thousands died from hunger, yet you Christians did nothing. You erect churches all through India, but the crying evil in the East is not religion — they have religion enough — but it is bread that the suffering millions of burning India cry out for with parched throats. They ask us for bread, but we give them stones. It is an insult to a starving people to offer them religion; it is an insult to a starving man to teach him metaphysics. In India a priest that preached for money would lose caste and be spat upon by the people. I came here to seek aid for my impoverished people, and I fully realised how difficult it was to get help for heathens from Christians in a Christian land.

Buddhism, The Fulfilment of Hinduism

26th September, 1893

I am not a Buddhist, as you have heard, and yet I am. If China, or Japan, or Ceylon follow the teachings of the Great Master, India worships him as God incarnate on earth. You have just now heard that I am going to criticise Buddhism, but by that I wish you to understand only this. Far be it from me to criticise him whom I worship as God incarnate on earth. But our views about Buddha are that he was not understood properly by his disciples. The relation between Hinduism (by Hinduism, I mean the religion of the Vedas) and what is called Buddhism at the present day is nearly the same as between Judaism and Christianity. Jesus Christ was a Jew, and Shâkya Muni was a Hindu. The Jews rejected Jesus Christ, nay, crucified him, and the Hindus have accepted Shâkya Muni as God and worship him. But the real difference that we Hindus want to show between modern Buddhism and what we should understand as the teachings of Lord Buddha lies principally in this: Shâkya Muni came to preach nothing new. He also, like Jesus, came to fulfil and not to destroy. Only, in the case of Jesus, it was the old people, the Jews, who did not understand him, while in the case of Buddha, it was his own followers who did not realise the import of his teachings. As the Jew did not understand the fulfilment of the Old Testament, so the Buddhist did not understand the fulfilment of the truths of the Hindu religion. Again, I repeat, Shâkya Muni came not to destroy, but he was the fulfilment, the logical conclusion, the logical development of the religion of the Hindus.

The religion of the Hindus is divided into two parts: the ceremonial and the spiritual. The spiritual portion is specially studied by the monks.

In that there is no caste. A man from the highest caste and a man from the lowest may become a monk in India, and the two castes become equal. In religion there is no caste; caste is simply a social institution. Shâkya Muni himself was a monk, and it was his glory that he had the large-heartedness to bring out the truths from the hidden Vedas and through them broadcast all over the world. He was the first being in the world who brought missionarising into practice — nay, he was the first to conceive the idea of proselytising.

The great glory of the Master lay in his wonderful sympathy for everybody, especially for the ignorant and the poor. Some of his disciples were Brahmins. When Buddha was teaching, Sanskrit was no more the spoken language in India. It was then only in the books of the learned. Some of Buddha's Brahmins disciples wanted to translate his teachings into Sanskrit, but he distinctly told them, "I am for the poor, for the people; let me speak in the tongue of the people." And so to this day the great bulk of his teachings are in the vernacular of that day in India.

Whatever may be the position of philosophy, whatever may be the position of metaphysics, so long as there is such a thing as death in the world, so long as there is such a thing as weakness in the human heart, so long as there is a cry going out of the heart of man in his very weakness, there shall be a faith in God.

On the philosophic side the disciples of the Great Master dashed themselves against the eternal rocks of the Vedas and could not crush them, and on the other side they took away from the nation that eternal God to which every one, man or woman, clings so fondly. And the result was that Buddhism had to die a natural death in India. At the present day there is not one who calls oneself a Buddhist in India, the land of its birth.

But at the same time, Brahminism lost something — that reforming zeal, that wonderful sympathy and charity for everybody, that wonderful heaven which Buddhism had brought to the masses and which had rendered Indian society so great that a Greek historian who wrote about India of that time was led to say that no Hindu was known to tell an untruth and no Hindu woman was known to be unchaste.

Hinduism cannot live without Buddhism, nor Buddhism without Hinduism. Then realise what the separation has shown to us, that the Buddhists cannot stand without the brain and philosophy of the Brahmins, nor the Brahmin without the heart of the Buddhist. This separation between the Buddhists and the Brahmins is the cause of the downfall of India. That is why India is populated by three hundred millions of beggars, and that is why India has been the slave of conquerors for the last thousand years. Let us then join the wonderful intellect of the Brahmins with the heart, the noble soul, the wonderful humanising power of the Great Master.

Address At the Final Session

27th September, 1893

The World's Parliament of Religions has become an accomplished fact, and the merciful Father has helped those who laboured to bring it into existence, and crowned with success their most unselfish labour.

My thanks to those noble souls whose large hearts and love of truth first dreamed this wonderful dream and then realised it. My thanks to the shower of liberal sentiments that has overflowed this platform. My thanks to his enlightened audience for their uniform kindness to me and for their appreciation of every thought that tends to smooth the friction of religions. A few jarring notes were heard from time to time in this harmony. My special thanks to them. for they have, by their striking contrast, made general harmony the sweeter.

Much has been said of the common ground of religious unity. I am not going just now to venture my own theory. But if any one here hopes that this unity will come by the triumph of any one of the religions and the destruction of the others, to him I say, "Brother, yours is an impossible hope." Do I wish that the Christian would become Hindu? God forbid. Do I wish that the Hindu or Buddhist would become Christian? God forbid.

The seed is put in the ground, and earth and air and water are placed around it. Does the seed become the earth; or the air, or the water? No. It becomes a plant, it develops after the law of its own growth, assimilates the air, the earth, and the water, converts them into plant substance, and grows into a plant.

Similar is the case with religion. The Christian is not to become a Hindu or a Buddhist, nor a Hindu or a Buddhist to become a Christian. But each must assimilate the spirit of the others and yet preserve his individuality and grow according to his own law of growth.

If the Parliament of Religions has shown anything to the world it is this: It has proved to the world that holiness, purity and charity are not the exclusive possessions of any church in the world, and that every system has produced men and women of the most exalted character. In the face of this evidence, if anybody dreams of the exclusive survival of his own religion and the destruction of the others, I pity him from the bottom of my heart, and point out to him that upon the banner of every religion will soon be written, in spite of resistance: "Help and not Fight," "Assimilation and not Destruction," "Harmony and Peace and not Dissension."

Bhakti or Devotion

The idea of a Personal God has obtained in almost every religion, except a very few. With the exception of the Buddhist and the Jain, perhaps all the religions of the world have the idea of a Personal God, and with it comes the idea of devotion and worship. The Buddhists and the Jains, although they have no Personal God, worship the founders of their religions in precisely the same way as others worship a Personal God.

This idea of devotion and worship to some higher being who can reflect back the love to man is universal. In various religions this love and devotion is manifested in various degrees, at different stages.

The lowest stage is that of ritualism, when abstract ideas are almost impossible, and are dragged down to the lowest plane, and made concrete. Forms come into play, and, along with them, various symbols.

Throughout the history of the world, we find that man is trying to grasp the abstract through thought-forms, or symbols. All the external manifestations of religion — bells, music, rituals, books, and images — come under that head. Anything that appeals to the senses, anything that helps man to form a concrete image of the abstract, is taken hold of, and worshipped.

From time to time, there have been reformers in every religion who have stood against all symbols and rituals. But vain has been their opposition, for so long as man will remain as he is, the vast majority will always want something concrete to hold on to, something around which, as it were, to place their ideas, something which will be the centre of all the thought-forms in their minds.

The great attempts of the Mohammedans and of the Protestants have been directed to this one end, of doing away with all rituals, and yet we find that even with them, rituals have crept in. They cannot be kept out; after long struggle, the masses simply change one symbol for another.

The Mohammedan, who thinks that every ritual, every form, image, or ceremony, used by a non-Mohammedan is sinful, does not think so when he comes to his own shrine, the Caaba. Every religious Mohammedan wherever he prays, must imagine that he is standing before the Caaba. When he makes a pilgrimage there, he must kiss the black stone in the wall of the shrine. All the kisses that have been imprinted on that stone, by millions and millions of pilgrims, will stand up as witnesses for the benefit of the faithful on the last day of judgment.

Then, there is the well of Zimzim. Mohammedans believe that whoever draws a little water out of that well will have his sins pardoned, and he will, after the day of resurrection, have a fresh body, and live for ever.

In others, we find that the symbology comes in the form of buildings. Protestants hold that churches are more sacred than other places. The church, as it is, stands for a symbol. Or there is the Book. The idea of the Book to them, is much holier than any other symbol.

It is vain to preach against the use of symbols, and why should we preach against them? There is no reason why man should not use symbols. They have them in order to represent the ideas signified behind them. This universe is a symbol, in and through which we are trying to grasp the thing signified, which is beyond and behind.

The spirit is the goal, and not matter. Forms, images, bells, candles, books, churches, temples, and all holy symbols are very good, very helpful to the growing plant of spirituality, but thus far and no farther.

In the test majority of cases, we find that the plant does not grow. It is very good to be born in a church, but it is very bad to die in a church. It is very good to be born within the limits of certain forms that help the little plant of spirituality, but if a man dies within the bounds of these forms, it shows that he has not grown, that there has been no development of the soul.

If, therefore, any one says that symbols, rituals, and forms are to be kept for ever, he is wrong; but if he says, that these symbols and rituals are a help to the growth of the soul, in its low and undeveloped state, he is right. But, you must not mistake this development of the soul as meaning anything intellectual. A man can be of gigantic intellect, yet spiritually he may be a baby.

You can verify it this moment. All of you have been taught to believe in an Omnipresent God. Try to think of it. How few of you can have any idea of what omnipresence means! If you struggle hard, you will get something like the idea of the ocean, or of the sky, or of a vast stretch of green earth, or of a desert.

All these are material images, and so long as you cannot conceive of the abstract as abstract, of the ideal as the ideal, you will have to resort to these forms, these material images. It does not make much difference whether these images are inside or outside the mind.

We are all born idolaters, and idolatry is good, because it is in the nature of man. Who can get beyond it? Only the perfect man, the God-man. The rest are all idolaters. So long as we see this universe before us, with its forms and shapes, we are all idolaters. This is a gigantic symbol we are worshipping.

He who says he is the body is a born idolater. We are spirit, spirit that has no form or shape, spirit that is infinite, and not matter. Therefore, anyone who cannot grasp the abstract, who cannot think of himself as he is, except in and through matter, as the body, is an idolater.

And yet how people fight among themselves, calling one another idolaters! In other words, each says, his idol is right, and the others' are wrong.

Therefore, we should get rid of these childish notions. We should get beyond the prattle of men who think that religion is merely a mass of frothy words, that it is only a system of doctrines; to whom religion is only a little intellectual assent or dissent; to whom religion is believing in certain words which their own priests tell them; to whom religion is something which their forefathers believed; to whom religion is a certain form of ideas and superstitions to which they cling because they are their national superstitions.

We should get beyond all these and look at humanity as one vast organism, slowly coming towards light — a wonderful plant, slowly unfolding itself to that wonderful truth which is called God — and the first gyrations, the first motions, towards this are always through matter and through ritual.

In the heart of all these ritualisms, there stands one idea prominent above all the rest — the worship of a name. Those of you who have studied the older forms of Christianity, those of you who have studied the other religions of the world, perhaps have marked that there is this idea with them all, the worship of a name.

A name is said to be very sacred. In the Bible we read that the holy name of God was considered sacred beyond compare, holy beyond everything. It was the holiest of all names, and it was thought that this very Word was God. This is quite true.

What is this universe but name and form? Can you think without words? Word and thought are inseparable. Try if any one of you can separate them. Whenever you think, you are doing so through word forms. The one brings the other; thought brings the word, and the word brings the thought.

Thus the whole universe is, as it were, the external symbol of God, and behind that stands His grand name. Each particular body is a form, and behind that particular body is its name.

As soon as you think of our friend So-and-so, there comes the idea of his body, and as soon as you think of your friend's body, you get the idea of his name. This is in the constitution of man.

That is to say, psychologically, in the mind-stuff of man, there cannot come the idea of name without the idea of form, and there cannot come the idea of form without the idea of name. They are inseparable; they are the external and the internal sides of the same wave. As such, names have been exalted and worshipped all over the world — consciously or unconsciously, man found the glory of names.

Again, we find that in many different religions, holy personages have been worshipped. They worship Krishna, they worship Buddha, they worship Jesus, and so forth.

Then, there is the worship of saints; hundreds of them have been worshipped all over the world, and why not? The vibration of light is everywhere. The owl sees it in the dark. That shows it is there, though man cannot see it.

To man, that vibration is only visible in the lamp, in the sun, in the moon, etc. God is omnipresent, He is manifesting Himself in every being; but for men, He is only visible, recognisable, in man. When His light, His presence, His spirit, shines through the human face, then and then alone, can man understand Him.

Thus, man has been worshipping God through men all the time, and must do so as long as he is a man. He may cry against it, struggle against it, but as soon as he attempts to realise God, he will find the constitutional necessity of thinking of God as a man.

So we find that in almost every religion these are the three primary things which we have in the worship of God — forms or symbols, names, God-men. All religions have these, but you find that they want to fight with each other.

One says, "My name is the only name; my form is the only form; and my God-men are the only God-men in the world; yours are simply myths."

In modern times, Christian clergymen have become a little kinder, and they allow that in the older religions, the different forms of worship were foreshadowings of Christianity, which of course, they consider, is the only true form. God tested Himself in older times, tested His powers by getting these things into shape which culminated in Christianity.

This, at least, is a great advance. Fifty years ago they would not have said even that; nothing was true except their own religion. This idea is not limited to any religion, nation, or class of persons; people are always thinking that the only right thing to be done by others is what they themselves are doing.

And it is here that the study of different religions helps us. It shows us that the same thoughts that we have been calling ours, and ours alone, were present hundreds of years ago in others, and sometimes even in a better form of expression than our own.

These are the external forms of devotion, through which man has to pass; but if he is sincere, if he really wants to reach the truth, he goes higher than these, to a plane where forms are as nothing. Temples or churches, books or forms, are simply the kindergarten of religion, to make the spiritual child strong enough to take higher steps; and these first steps are necessary if he wants religion.

With the thirst, the longing for God, comes real devotion, real Bhakti. Who has the longing? That is the question. Religion is not in doctrines, in dogmas, nor in intellectual argumentation; it is being and becoming, it is realisation.

We hear so many talking about God and the soul, and all the mysteries of the universe, but if you take them one by one, and ask them, "Have you realised God? Have you seen your Soul?" — how many can say they have? And yet they are all fighting with one another!

At one time, in India, representatives of different sects met together and began to dispute. One said that the only God was Shiva; another said, the only God was Vishnu, and so on; and there was no end to their discussion.

A sage was passing that way, and was invited by the disputants to decide the matter. He first asked the man who was claiming Shiva as the greatest God, "Have you seen Shiva? Are you acquainted with Him? If not, how do you know He is the greatest God?"

Then turning to the worshipper of Vishnu, he asked, "Have you seen Vishnu?"

And after asking this question to all of them, he found out that not one of them knew anything of God. That was why they were disputing so much, for had they really known, they would not have argued.

When a jar is being filled with water, it makes a noise, but when it is full, there is no noise. So, the very fact of these disputations and fighting among sects shows that they do not know anything about religion. Religion to them is a mere mass of frothy words, to be written in books.

Each one hurries to write a big book, to make it as massive as possible, stealing his materials from every book he can lay his hands upon, and never acknowledging his indebtedness. Then he launches this book upon the world, adding to the disturbance that is already existing there.

The vast majority of men are atheists. I am glad that, in modern times, another class of atheists has come into existence in the Western world — I mean the materialists. They are sincere atheists. They are better than the religious atheists, who are insincere, who fight and talk about religion, and yet do not want it, never try to realise it, never try to understand it.

Remember the words of Christ: "Ask, and it shall be given you; seek, and ye shall find; knock, and it shall be opened unto you." These words are literally true, not figures or fiction. They were the outflow of the heart's blood of one of the greatest sons of God who have ever come to this world of ours; words which came as the fruit of realisation, from a man who had felt and realised God himself; who had spoken with God, lived with God, a hundred times more intensely than you or I see this building.

Who wants God? That is the question. Do you think that all this mass of people in the world want God, and cannot get Him? That cannot be. What want is there without its object outside? Man wants to breathe, and there is air for him to breathe. Man wants to eat, and there is food to eat.

What creates these desires? The existence of external things. It was the light that made the eyes; it was the sound that made the ears.

So every desire in human beings has been created by something which already existed outside. This desire for perfection, for reaching the goal and getting beyond nature, how can it be there, until something has created it and drilled it into the soul of man, and makes it live there? He, therefore, in whom this desire is awakened, will reach the goal.

We want everything but God. This is not religion that you see all around you. My lady has furniture in her parlour, from all over the world, and now it is the fashion to have something Japanese; so she buys a vase and puts it in her room. Such is religion with the vast majority; they have all sorts of things for enjoyment, and unless they add a little flavour of religion, life is not all right, because society would criticise them. Society expects it; so they must have some religion. This is the present state of religion in the world.

A disciple went to his master and said to him, "Sir, I want religion." The master looked at the young man, and did not speak, but only smiled.

The young man came every day, and insisted that he wanted religion. But the old man knew better than the young man.

One day, when it was very hot, he asked the young man to go to the river with him and take a plunge. The young man plunged in, and the old man followed him and held the young man down under the water by force. After the young man had struggled for a while, he let him go and asked him what he wanted most while he was under the water.

"A breath of air", the disciple answered.

"Do you want God in that way? If you do, you will get Him in a moment," said the master.

Until you have that thirst, that desire, you cannot get religion, however you may struggle with your intellect, or your books, or your forms. Until that thirst is awakened in you, you are no better than any atheist; only the atheist is sincere, and you are not.

A great sage used to say, "Suppose there is a thief in a room, and somehow he comes to know that there is a vast mass of gold in the next room, and that there is only a thin partition between the two rooms What would be the condition of that thief? He would be sleepless, he would not be able to eat or do anything. His whole mind would be on getting that gold. Do you mean to say that, if all these people really believed that the Mine of Happiness, of Blessedness, of Glory were here, they would act as they do in the world, without trying to get God?"

As soon as a man begins to believe there is a God, he becomes mad with longing to get to Him. Others may go their way, but as soon as a man is sure that there is a much higher life than that which he is leading here, as soon as he feels sure that the senses are not all, that this limited, material body is as nothing compared with the immortal, eternal, undying bliss of the Self, he becomes mad until he finds out this bliss for himself.

And this madness, this thirst, this mania, is what is called the "awakening" to religion, and when that has come, a man is beginning to be religious. But it takes a long time. All these forms and ceremonies, these prayers and pilgrimages, these books, bells, candles, and priests, are the preparations; they take off the impurities from the soul.

And when the soul has become pure, it naturally wants to get to the mine of all purity, God Himself. Just as a piece of iron, which had been covered with the dust of centuries, might be lying near a magnet all the time, and yet not be attracted by it, but as soon as the dust is cleared away, the iron is drawn by the magnet; so, when the human soul, covered with the dust of ages, impurities, wickednesses, and sins, after many births, becomes purified enough by these forms and ceremonies, by doing good to others, loving other beings, its natural spiritual attraction comes, it wakes up and struggles towards God.

Yet, all these forms and symbols are simply the beginning, not true love of God. Love we hear spoken of everywhere Everyone says, "Love God." Men do not know what it into love; if they did, they would not talk so glibly about it. Every man says he can love, and then, in no time, finds out that there is no love in his nature. Every woman says she can love and soon finds out that she cannot. The world is full of the talk of love, but it is hard to love.

Where is love? How do you know that there is love? The first test of love is that it knows no bargaining. So long as you see a man love another only to get something from him, you know that that is not love; it is shopkeeping. Wherever there is any question of buying and selling, it is not love.

So, when a man prays to God, "Give me this, and give me that", it is not love. How can it be? I offer you a prayer, and you give me something in return; that is what it is, mere shopkeeping.

A certain great king went to hunt in a forest, and there he happened to meet a sage. He had a little conversation with him and became so pleased with him that he asked him to accept a present from him.

"No," said the sage, "I am perfectly satisfied with my condition; these trees give me enough fruit to eat; these beautiful pure streams supply me with all the water I want; I sleep in these caves. What do I care for your presents, though you be an emperor?"

The emperor said, "Just to purify me, to gratify me, come with me into the city and take some present."

At last the sage consented to go with the emperor, and he was taken into the emperor's palace, where there were gold, jewellery, marble, and most wonderful things. Wealth and power were manifest everywhere. The emperor asked the sage to wait a minute, while he repeated his prayer, and he went into a corner and began to pray, "Lord, give me more wealth, more children, more territory."

In the meanwhile, the sage got up and began to walk away. The emperor saw him going and went after him. "Stay, Sir, you did not take my present and are going away."

The sage turned to him and said, "Beggar, I do not beg of beggars. What can you give? You have been begging yourself all the time."

That is not the language of love. What is the difference between love and shopkeeping, if you ask God to give you this, and give you that? The first test of love is that it knows no bargaining. Love is always the giver, and never the taker.

Says the child of God, "If God wants, I give Him my everything, but I do not want anything of Him. I want nothing in this universe. I love Him, because I want to love Him, and I ask no favour in return. Who cares whether God is almighty or not? I do not want any power from Him nor any manifestation of His power. Sufficient for me that He is the God of love. I ask no more question."

The second test is that love knows no fear. So long as man thinks of God as a Being sitting above the clouds, with rewards in one hand and punishments in the other, there can be no love.

Can you frighten one into love? Does the lamb love the lion? The mouse, the cat? The slave, the master? Slaves sometimes simulate love, but is it love? Where do you ever see love in fear? It is always a sham. With love never comes the idea of fear.

Think of a young mother in the street: if a dog barks at her, she flees into the nearest house. The next day she is in the street with her child, and suppose a lion rushes upon the child, where will be her position? Just at the mouth of the lion, protecting her child. Love conquered all her fear.

So also in the love of God. Who cares whether God is a rewarder or a punisher? That is not the thought of a lover. Think of a judge when he comes home, what does his wife see in him? Not a judge, or a rewarder or punisher, but her husband, her love. What do his children see in him? Their loving father, not the punisher or rewarder.

So the children of God never see in Him a punisher or a rewarder. It is only people who have never tasted of love that fear and quake. Cast off all fear — though these horrible ideas of God as a punisher or rewarder may have their use in savage minds.

Some men, even the most intellectual, are spiritual savages, and these ideas may help them. But to men who are spiritual, men who are approaching religion, in whom spiritual insight is awakened, such ideas are simply childish, simply foolish. Such men reject all ideas of fear.

The third is a still higher test. Love is always the highest ideal. When one has passed through the first two stages, when one has thrown off all shopkeeping, and cast off all fear, one then begins to realise that love is always the highest ideal.

How many times in this world we see a beautiful woman loving an ugly man? How many times we see a handsome man loving an ugly woman! What is the attraction? Lookers-on only see the ugly man or the ugly woman, but not so the lover; to the lover the beloved is the most beautiful being that ever existed. How is it? The woman who loves the ugly man takes, as it were, the ideal of beauty which is in her own mind, and projects it on this ugly man; and what she worships and loves is not the ugly man, but her own ideal. That man is, as it were, only the suggestion, and upon that suggestion she throws her own ideal, and covers it; and it becomes her object of worship.

Now, this applies in every case where we love. Many of us have very ordinary looking brothers or sisters; yet the very idea of their being brothers or sisters makes them beautiful to us.

The philosophy in the background is that each one projects his own ideal and worships that. This external world is only the world of suggestion. All that we see, we project out of our own minds.

A grain of sand gets washed into the shell of an oyster and irritates it. The irritation produces a secretion in the oyster, which covers the grain of sand and the beautiful pearl is the result.

Similarly, external things furnish us with suggestions, over which we project our own ideals and make our objects. The wicked see this world as a perfect hell, and the good as a perfect heaven. Lovers see this world as full of love, and haters as full of hatred; fighters see nothing but strife, and the peaceful nothing but peace.

The perfect man sees nothing but God. So we always worship our highest ideal, and when we have reached the point, when we love the ideal as the ideal, all arguments and doubts vanish for ever.

Who cares whether God can be demonstrated or not? The ideal can never go, because it is a part of my own nature. I shall only question the ideal when I question my own existence, and as I cannot question the one, I cannot question the other.

Who cares whether God can be almighty and all-merciful at the same time or not? Who cares whether He is the rewarder of mankind, whether He looks at us with the eyes of a tyrant or with the eyes of a beneficent monarch?

The lover has passed beyond all these things, beyond rewards and punishments, beyond fears and doubts, beyond scientific or any other demonstration. Sufficient unto him is the ideal of love, and is it not self-evident that this universe is but a manifestation of this love? What is it that makes atoms unite with atoms, molecules with molecules, and causes planets to fly towards each other? What is it that attracts man to man, man to woman, woman to man, and animals to animals, drawing the whole universe, as it were, towards one centre?

It is what is called love. Its manifestation is from the lowest atom to the highest being: omnipotent, all-pervading, is this love. What manifests itself as attraction in the sentient and the insentient, in the particular and in the universal, is the love of God. It is the one motive power that is in the universe.

Under the impetus of that love, Christ gives his life for humanity, Buddha even for an animal, the mother for the child, the husband for the wife. It is under the impetus of the same love that men are ready to give up their lives for their country, and strange to say, under the impetus of the same love, the thief steals, the murderer murders. Even in these cases, the spirit is the same, but the manifestation is different. This is the one motive power in the universe.

The thief has love for gold; the love is there, but it is misdirected. So, in all crimes, as well as in all virtuous actions, behind stands that eternal love.

Suppose a man writes a cheque for a thousand dollars for the poor of New York, and at the same time, in the same room, another man forges the name of a friend. The light by which both of them write is the same, but each one will be responsible for the use he makes of it. It is not the light that is to be praised or blamed. Unattached, yet shining in everything, is love, the motive power of the universe, without which the universe would fall to pieces in a moment, and this love is God.

"None, O beloved, loves the husband for the husband's sake, but for the Self that is in the husband; none, O beloved, ever loves the wife for the wife's sake, but for the Self that is in the wife. None ever loves anything else, except for the Self."

Even this selfishness, which is so much condemned, is but a manifestation of the same love. Stand aside from this play, do not mix in it, but see this wonderful panorama, this grand drama, played scene after scene, and hear this wonderful harmony; all are the manifestation of the same love. Even in selfishness, that self will multiply, grow and grow.

That one self, the one man, will become two selves when he gets married; several, when he gets children; and thus he grows until he feels the whole world as his Self, the whole universe as his Self. He expands into one mass of universal love, infinite love — the love that is God.

Thus we come to what is called supreme Bhakti, supreme devotion, in which forms and symbols fall off. One who has reached that cannot belong to any sect, for all sects are in him.

To what shall he belong? For all churches and temples are in him. Where is the church big enough for him? Such a man cannot bind himself down to certain limited forms. Where is the limit for unlimited love, with which he has become one? In all religions which take up this ideal of love, we find the struggle to express it.

Although we understand what this love means and see that everything in this world of affections and attractions is a manifestation of that Infinite Love, the expression of which has been attempted by sages and saints of different nations, yet we find them using all the powers of language, transfiguring even the most carnal expression into the divine.

Thus sang the royal Hebrew sage, thus sang they of India. "O beloved, one kiss of Thy lips! Kissed by Thee, one's thirst for Thee increaseth for ever! All sorrows cease, one forgets the past, present, and future, and only thinks of Thee alone."

That is the madness of the lover, when all desires have vanished. "Who cares for salvation? Who cares to be saved? Who cares to be perfect even? Who cares for freedom?" — says the lover. "I do not want wealth, nor even health; I do not want beauty, I do not want intellect: let me be born again and again, amid all the evils that are in the world; I will not complain, but let me love Thee, and that for love's sake."

That is the madness of love which finds expression in these songs. The highest, most expressive, strongest, and most attractive human love is that between man and woman, and, therefore, that language was used in expressing the deepest devotion. The madness of this human love was the faintest echo of the mad love of the saints.

The true lovers of God want to become mad, inebriated with the love of God, to become "God-intoxicated men". They want to drink of the cup of love which has been prepared by the saints and sages of every religion, who have poured their heart's blood into it, and in which hare been concentrated all the hopes of those who have loved God without seeking reward, who wanted love for itself only.

The reward of love is love, and what a reward it is! It is the only thing that takes off all sorrows, the only cup, by the drinking of which this disease of the world vanishes Man becomes divinely mad and forgets that be is man.

Lastly, we find that all these various systems, in the end, converge to that one point, that perfect union. We always begin as dualists. God is a separate Being, and I am a separate being.

Love comes between, and man begins to approach God, and God, as it were, begins to approach man. Man takes up all the various relationships of life, as father, mother, friend, or lover; and the last point is reached when he becomes one with the object of worship.

"I am you, and you are I; and worshipping you, I worship myself; and in worshipping myself, I worship you."

There we find the highest culmination of that with which man begins. At the beginning it was love for the self, but the claims of the little self made love selfish; at the end came the full blaze of light, when that self had become the Infinite.

That God who at first was a Being somewhere, became resolved, as it were, into Infinite Love. Man himself was also transformed. He was approaching God, he was throwing off all vain desires, of which he was full before. With desires vanished selfishness, and, at the apex, he found that Love, Lover, and Beloved were One.

Krishna

This article was recorded by Ida Ansell in shorthand. As, however, Swamiji's speed was too great for her in her early days, dots are put in the articles to indicate the omissions, while the words within square brackets are added by way of linking up the disconnected parts.

(Delivered in California, on April 1, 1900)

Almost the same circumstances which gave birth to Buddhism in India surrounded the rise of Krishna. Not only this, the events of that day we find happening in our own times.

There is a certain ideal. At the same time there must always be a large majority of the human race who cannot come up to the ideal, not even intellectually. ... The strong ones carry it out and many times have no sympathy for the weak. The weak to the strong are only beggars. The strong ones march ahead. ... Of course, we see at once that the highest position to take is to be sympathetic and helpful to those who are weak. But then, in many cases the philosopher bars the way to our being sympathetic. If we go by the theory that the whole of this infinite life has to be determined by the few years' existence here and now, ... then it is very hopeless for us, ... and we have no time to look back upon those who are weak. But if these are not the conditions — if the world is only one of the many schools through which we have to pass, if the eternal life is to be moulded and fashioned and guided by the eternal law, and eternal law, eternal chances await everyone — then we need not be in a hurry. We have time to sympathise, to look around, stretch out a helping hand to the weak and bring them up.

With Buddhism we have two words in Sanskrit: one is translated religion, the other, a sect. It is the most curious fact that the disciples and descendants of Krishna have no name for their religion [although] foreigners call it Hinduism or Brâhmanism. There is one religion, and there are many sects. The moment you give it a name, individualise it and separate it from the rest, it is a sect, no more a religion. A sect [proclaims] its own truth and declares that there is no truth anywhere else. Religion believes that there has been, and still is, one religion in the world. There never were two religions. It is the same religion [presenting] different aspects in different places. The task is to conceive the proper understanding of the goal and scope of humanity.

This was the great work of Krishna: to clear our eyes and make us look with broader vision upon humanity in its march upward and onward. His was the first heart that was large enough to see truth in all, his the first lips that uttered beautiful words for each and all.

This Krishna preceded Buddha by some thousand years. ... A great many people do not believe that he ever existed. Some believe that [the worship of Krishna grew out of] the old sun worship. There seem to be several Krishnas: one was mentioned in the Upanishads, another was king, another a general. All have been lumped into one Krishna. It does not matter much. The fact is, some individual comes who is unique in spirituality. Then all sorts of legends are invented around him. But, all the Bibles and stories which come to be cast upon this one person have to be recast in [the mould of] his character. All the stories of the New Testament have to be modelled upon the accepted life [and] character of Christ. In all of the Indian stories about Buddha the one central note of that whole life is kept up — sacrifice for others. ...

In Krishna we find ... two ideas [stand] supreme in his message: The first is the harmony of different ideas; the second is non-attachment. A man can attain to perfection, the highest goal, sitting on a throne, commanding armies, working out big plans for nations. In fact, Krishna's great sermon was preached on the battlefield.

Krishna saw plainly through the vanity of all the mummeries, mockeries, and ceremonials of the old priests; and yet he saw some good in them.

If you are a strong man, very good! But do not curse others who are not strong enough for you. ... Everyone says, "Woe unto you people! !" Who says, "Woe unto me that I cannot help you?" The people are doing all right to the best of their ability and means and knowledge. Woe unto me that I cannot lift them to where I am!

So the ceremonials, worship of gods, and myths, are all right, Krishna says. ... Why? Because they all lead to the same goal. Ceremonies, books, and forms— all these are links in the chain. Get hold! That is the one thing. If you are sincere and have really got hold of one link, do not let go; the rest is bound to come. [But people] do not get hold. They spend the time quarrelling and determining what they should get hold of, and do not get hold of anything. ... We are always after truth, but never want to get it. We simply want the pleasure to go about and ask. We have a lot of energy and spend it that way. That is why Krishna says: Get hold of any one of these chains that are stretched out from the common centre. No one step is greater than another. ... Blame no view of religion so far as it is sincere. Hold on to one of these links, and it will pull you to the centre. Your heart itself will teach all the rest. The teacher within will teach all the creeds, all the philosophies. ...

Krishna talks of himself as God, as Christ does. He sees the Deity in himself. And he says, "None can go a day out of my path. All have to come to me. Whosoever wants to worship in whatsoever form, I give him faith in that form, and through that I meet him. ..."(Gita, IV. 12.) His heart is all for the masses.

Independent, Krishna stands out. The very boldness of it frightens us. We depend upon everything — ... upon a few good words, upon circumstances. When the soul wants to depend upon nothing, not even upon life, that is the height of philosophy, the height of manhood. Worship leads to the same goal. Krishna lays great stress upon worship. Worship God!

Various sorts of worship we see in this world. The sick man is very worshipful to God. ... There is the man who loses his fortune; he also prays very much, to get money. The highest worship is that of the man who loves God for God's sake. [The question may be asked :] "Why should there be so much sorrow if there is a God?" The worshipper replies! " ... There is misery in the world; [but] because of that I do not cease to love God. I do not worship Him to take away my [misery]. I love Him because He is love itself." The other [types of worship] are lower-grade; but Krishna has no condemnation for anything. It is better to do something than to stand still. The man who begins to worship God will grow by degrees and begin to love God for love's sake. ...

How to attain purity living this life? Shall we all go to the forest caves? What good would it do? If the mind is not under control, it is no use living in a cave because the same mind will bring all disturbances there. We will find twenty devils in the cave because all the devils are in the mind. If the mind is under control, we can have the cave anywhere, wherever we are.

It is our own mental attitude which makes the world what it is for us. Our thoughts make things beautiful, our thoughts make things ugly. The whole world is in our own minds. Learn to see things in the proper light. First, believe in this world — that there is meaning behind everything. Everything in the world is good, is holy and beautiful. If you see something evil, think that you are not understanding it in the right light. Throw the burden on yourselves! ... Whenever we are tempted to say that the world is going to the dogs, we ought to analyse ourselves, and we shall find that we have lost the faculty of seeing things as they are.

Work day and night! "Behold, I am the Lord of the Universe. I have no duty. Every duty is bondage. But I work for work's sake. If I ceased to work for a minute, [there would be chaos]."(Ibid. III. 22-23.) So do thou work, without any idea of duty. ...

This world is a play. You are His playmates. Go on and work, without any sorrow, without any misery. See His play in the slums, in the saloons! Work to lift people! Not that they are vile or degraded; Krishna does not say that.

Do you know why so little good work is done? My lady goes to the slum. ... She gives a few ducats and says, "My poor men, take that and be happy!" ... Or my fine woman, walking through the street, sees a poor fellow and throws him five cents. Think of the blasphemy of it! Blessed are we that the Lord has given us his teaching in your own Testament. Jesus says, "Inasmuch as ye have done it unto the least of these my brethren, ye have done it unto me." It is blasphemy to think that you can help anyone. First root out this idea of helping, and then go to worship. God's children are your Master's children. [And children are but different forms of the father.] You are His servant ... Serve the living God! God comes to you in the blind, in the halt, in the poor, in the weak, in the diabolical. What a glorious chance for you to worship! The moment you think you are "helping", you undo the whole thing and degrade yourself. Knowing this, work. "What follows?" you say. You do not get that heartbreak, that awful misery. ... Then work is no more slavery. It becomes a play, and joy itself. ... Work! Be unattached! That is the whole secret. If you get attached, you become miserable. ...

With everything we do in life we identify ourselves. Here is a man who says harsh words to me. I feel anger coming on me. In a few seconds anger and I are one, and then comes misery. Attach yourselves to the Lord and to nothing else, because everything else is unreal. Attachment to the unreal will bring misery. There is only one Existence that is real, only one Life in which there is neither object nor [subject]. ...

But unattached love will not hurt you. Do anything — marry, have children. ... Do anything you like — nothing will hurt you. Do nothing with the idea of "mine". Duty for duty's sake; work for work's sake. What is that to you? You stand aside.

When we come to that non-attachment, then we can understand the marvellous mystery of the universe; how it is intense activity and vibration, and at the same time intensest peace and calm; how it is work every moment and rest every moment. That is the mystery of the universe — the impersonal and personal in one, the infinite and finite in one. Then we shall find the secret. "He who finds in the midst of intense activity the greatest rest, and in the midst of the greatest rest intense activity, he has become a Yogi." (Ibid. IV. 18.) He alone is a real worker, none else. We do a little work and break ourselves. Why? We become attached to that work. If we do not become attached, side by side with it we have infinite rest. ...

How hard it is to arrive at this sort of non-attachment! Therefore Krishna shows us the lower ways and methods. The easiest way for everyone is to do [his or her] work and not take the results. It is our desire that binds us. If we take the results of actions, whether good or evil, we will have to bear them. But if we work not for ourselves, but all for the glory of the Lord, the results will take care of themselves. "To work you have the right, but not to the fruits thereof." (Ibid. II. 47.) The soldier works for no results. He does his duty. If defeat comes, it belongs to the general, not to the soldier. We do our duty for love's sake — love for the general, love for the Lord. ...

If you are strong, take up the Vedanta philosophy and be independent. If you cannot do that, worship God; if not, worship some image. If you lack strength even to do that, do some good works without the idea of gain. Offer everything you have unto the service of the Lord. Fight on! "Leaves and water and one flower — whosoever lays anything on my altar, I receive it with equal delights."(Ibid IX. 26.) If you cannot do anything, not a single good work, then take refuge [in the Lord]. "The Lord resides within the heart of the being, making them turn upon His wheel. Do thou with all thy soul and heart take refuge in Him. ...(Ibid XVIII. 61-62.)

These are some of the general ideas that Krishna preached on this idea of love [in the Gita]. There are [in] other great books, sermons on love — as with Buddha, as with Jesus. ...

A few words about the life of Krishna. There is a great deal of similarity between the lives of Jesus and Krishna. A discussion is going on as to which borrowed of the other. There was the tyrannical king in both places. Both were born in a manger. The parents were bound in both cases. Both were saved by angels. In both cases all the boys born in that year were killed. The childhood is the same. ... Again, in the end, both were killed. Krishna was killed by accident; he took the man who killed him to heaven. Christ was killed, and blessed the robber and took him to heaven.

There are a great many similarities in of the New Testament and the Gita. The human thought goes the same way. ... I will find you the answer in the words of Krishna himself: "Whenever virtue subsides and irreligion prevails, I come down. Again and again I come. Therefore, whenever thou seest a great soul struggling to uplift mankind, know that I am come, and worship. ..."(Ibid. IV. 8; X. 41.)

At the same time, if he comes as Jesus or as Buddha, why is there so much schism? The preachings must be followed! A Hindu devotee would say: It is God himself who became Christ and Krishna and Buddha and all these [great teachers]. A Hindu philosopher would say: These are the great souls; they are already free. And though free, they refuse to accept their liberation while the whole world is suffering. They come again and again, take a human embodiment and help mankind. They know from their childhood what they are and what they come for. ... They do not come through bondage like we do. ... They come out of their own free will, and cannot help having tremendous spiritual power. We cannot resist it. The vast mass of mankind is dragged into the whirlpool of spirituality, and the vibration goes on and on because one of these [great souls] gives a push. So it continues until all mankind is liberated and the play of this planet is finished.

Glory unto the great souls whose lives we have been studying! They are the living gods of the world. They are the persons whom we ought to worship. If He comes to me, I can only recognise Him if He takes a human form. He is everywhere, but do we see Him? We can only see Him if He takes the limitation of man. .... If men and ... animals are manifestations of God, these teachers of mankind are leaders, are Gurus. Therefore, salutations unto you, whose footstool is worshipped by angels! Salutations unto you leaders of the human race! Salutations unto you great teachers! You leaders have our salutations for ever and ever!

The Soul and God

This article was recorded by Ida Ansell in shorthand. As, however, Swamiji's speed was too great for her in her early days, dots are put in the articles to indicate the omissions, while the words within square brackets are added by way of linking up the disconnected parts.

(Delivered in San Francisco, March 23, 1900)

Whether it was fear or mere inquisitiveness which first led man to think of powers superior to himself, we need not discuss. ... These raised in the mind peculiar worship tendencies, and so on. There never have been [times in the history of mankind] without [some ideal] of worship. Why? What makes us all struggle for something beyond what we see — whether it be a beautiful morning or a fear of dead spirits? ... We need not go back into prehistoric times, for it is a fact present today as it was two thousand years ago. We do not find satisfaction here. Whatever our station in life — [even if we are] powerful and wealthy — we cannot find satisfaction.

Desire is infinite. Its fulfilment is very limited.. There is no end to our desires; but when we go to fulfil them, the difficulty comes. It has been so with the most primitive minds, when their desires were [few]. Even [these] could not be accomplished. Now, with our arts and sciences improved and multiplied, our desires cannot be fulfilled [either]. On the other hand, we are struggling to perfect means for the fulfilment of desires, and the desires are increasing. ...

The most primitive man naturally wanted help from outside for things which he could not accomplish. ...He desired something, and it could not be obtained. He wanted help from other powers. The most ignorant primitive man and the most cultivated man today, each appealing to God and asking for the fulfilment of some desire, are exactly the same. What difference? [Some people] find a great deal of difference. We are always finding much difference in things when there is no difference at all. Both [the primitive man and the cultivated man] plead to the same [power]. You may call it God or Allah or Jehovah. Human beings want something and cannot get it by their own powers, and are after someone who will help them. This is primitive, and it is still present with us. ... We are all born savages and gradually civilise ourselves. ... All of us here, if we search, will find the same fact. Even now this fear does not leave us. We may talk big, become philosophers and all that; but when the blow comes, we find that we must beg for help. We believe in all the superstitions that ever existed. [But] there is no superstition in the world [that does not have some basis of truth]. If I cover my face and only the tip of my [nose] is showing, still it is a bit of my face. So [with] the superstitions — the little bits are true.

You see, the lowest sort of manifestation of religion came with the burial of the departed. ... First they wrapped them up and put them in mounds, and the spirits of the departed came and lived in the [mounds, at night]. ... Then they began to bury them. ... At the gate stands a terrible goddess with a thousand teeth. ... Then [came] the burning of the body and the flames bore the spirit up. ... The Egyptians brought food and water for the departed.

The next great idea was that of the tribal gods. This tribe had one god and that tribe another. The Jews had their God Jehovah, who was their own tribal god and fought against all the other gods and tribes. That god would do anything to please his own people. If he killed a whole tribe not protected by him, that was all right, quite good. A little love was given, but that love was confined to a small section.

Gradually, higher ideals came. The chief of the conquering tribe was the Chief of chiefs, God of gods. ... So with the Persians when they conquered Egypt. The Persian emperor was the Lord of [lords], and before the emperor nobody could stand. Death was the penalty for anyone who looked at the Persian emperor.

Then came the ideal of God Almighty and All-powerful, the omnipotent, omniscient Ruler of the universe: He lives in heaven, and man pays special tribute to his Most Beloved, who creates everything for man. The whole world is for man. The sun and moon and stars are [for him]. All who have those ideas are primitive men, not civilised and not cultivated at all. All the superior religions had their growth between the Ganga and the Euphrates. ... Outside of India we will find no further development [of religion beyond this idea of God in heaven]. That was the highest knowledge ever obtained outside of India. There is the local heaven where he is and [where] the faithful shall go when they die. ... As far as I have seen, we should call it a very primitive idea. ... Mumbo jumbo in Africa [and] God in heaven — the same. He moves the world, and of course his will is being done everywhere. ...

The old Hebrew people did not care for any heaven. That is one of the reasons they [opposed] Jesus of Nazareth — because he taught life after death. Paradise in Sanskrit means land beyond this life. So the paradise was to make up for all this evil. The primitive man does not care [about] evil. ... He never questions why there should be any. ...

... The word devil is a Persian word. ... The Persians and Hindus [share the Aryan ancestry] upon religious grounds, and ... they spoke the same language, only the words one sect uses for good the other uses for bad. The word Deva is an old Sanskrit word for God, the same word in the Aryan languages. Here the word means the devil. ...

Later on, when man developed [his inner life], he began to question, and to say that God is good. The Persians said that there were two gods — one was bad and one was good. [Their idea was that] everything in this life was good: beautiful country, where there was spring almost the whole year round and nobody died; there was no disease, everything was fine. Then came this Wicked One, and he touched the land, and then came death and disease and mosquitoes and tigers and lions. Then the Aryans left their fatherland and migrated southward. The old Aryans must have lived way to the north. The Jews learnt it [the idea of the devil] from the Persians. The Persians also taught that there will come a day when this wicked god will be killed, and it is our duty to stay with the good god and add our force to him in this eternal struggle between him and the wicked one. ... The whole world will be burnt out and everyone will get a new body.

The Persian idea was that even the wicked will be purified and not be bad any more. The nature of the Aryan was love and poetry. They cannot think of their being burnt [for eternity]. They will all receive new bodies. Then no more death. So that is the best about [religious] ideas outside of India. ...

Along with that is the ethical strain. All that man has to do is to take care of three things: good thought, good word, good deed. That is all. It is a practical, wise religion. Already there has come a little poetry in it. But there is higher poetry and higher thought.

In India we see this Satan in the most ancient part of the Vedas. He just (appears) and immediately disappears. ... In the Vedas the bad god got a blow and disappeared. He is gone, and the Persians took him. We are trying to make him leave the world [al]together. Taking the Persian idea, we are going to make a decent gentleman of him; give him a new body. There was the end of the Satan idea in India.

But the idea of God went on; but mind you, here comes another fact. The idea of God grew side by side with the idea of [materialism] until you have traced it up to the emperor of Persia. But on the other hand comes in metaphysics, philosophy. There is another line of thought, the idea of [the non-dual Âtman, man's] own soul. That also grows. So, outside of India ideas about God had to remain in that concrete form until India came to help them out a bit. ... The other nations stopped with that old concrete idea. In this country [America], there are millions who believe that God is [has?] a body. ...

Whole sects say it. [They believe that] He rules the world, but there is a place where He has a body. He sits upon a throne. They light candles and sing songs just as they do in our temples.

But in India they are sensible enough never to make [their God a physical being]. You never see in India a temple of Brahmâ. Why? Because the idea of the soul always existed. The Hebrew race never questioned about the soul. There is no soul idea in the Old Testament at all. The first is in the New Testament. The Persians, they became so practical — wonderfully practical people — a fighting, conquering race. They were the English people of the old time, always fighting and destroying their neighbours — too much engaged in that sort of thing to think about the soul. ...

The oldest idea of [the] soul [was that of] a fine body inside this gross one. The gross one disappears and the fine one appears. In Egypt that fine one also dies, and as soon as the gross body disintegrates, the fine one also disintegrates. That is why they built those pyramids [and embalmed the dead bodies of their ancestors, thus hoping to secure immortality for the departed]. ...

The Indian people have no regard for the dead body at all. [Their attitude is:] "Let us take it and burn it." The son has to set fire to his father's body. ...

There are two sorts of races, the divine and the demonic. The divine think that they are soul and spirit. The demonic think that they are bodies. The old Indian philosophers tried to insist that the body is nothing. "As a man emits his old garment and takes a new one, even so the old body is [shed] and he takes a new one" (Gita, II. 22). In my case, all my surrounding and education were trying to [make me] the other way. I was always associated with Mohammedans and Christians, who take more care of the body. ...

It is only one step from [the body] to the spirit. ... [In India] they became insistent on this ideal of the soul. It became [synonymous with] the idea of God. ... If the idea of the soul begins to expand, [man must arrive at the conclusion that it is beyond name and form]. ... The Indian idea is that the soul is formless. Whatever is form must break some time or other. There cannot be any form unless it is the result of force and matter; and all combinations must dissolve. If such is the case, [if] your soul is [made of name and form, it disintegrates], and you die, and you are no more immortal. If it is double, it has form and it belongs to nature and it obeys nature's laws of birth and death. ... They find that this [soul] is not the mind ... neither a double. ...

Thoughts can be guided and controlled. ... [The Yogis of India] practiced to see how far the thoughts can be guided and controlled. By dint of hard work, thoughts may be silenced altogether. If thoughts were [the real man], as soon as thought ceases, he ought to die. Thought ceases in meditation; even the mind's elements are quite quiet. Blood circulation stops. His breath stops, but he is not dead. If thought were he, the whole thing ought to go, but they find it does not go. That is practical [proof].

They came to the conclusion that even mind and thought were not the real man. Then speculation showed that it could not be.

I come, I think and talk. In the midst of all [this activity is] this unity [of the Self]. My thought and action are varied, many [fold] ... but in and through them runs ... that one unchangeable One. It cannot be the body. That is changing every minute. It cannot be the mind; new and fresh thoughts [come] all the time. It is neither the body nor the mind. Both body and mind belong to nature and must obey nature's laws. A free mind never will. ...

Now, therefore, this real man does not belong to nature. It is the person whose mind and body belong to nature. So much of nature we are using. Just as you come to use the pen and ink and chair, so he uses so much of nature in fine and in gross form; gross form, the body, and fine form, the mind. If it is simple, it must be formless. In nature alone are forms. That which is not of nature cannot have any forms, fine or gross. It must be formless. It must be omnipresent. Understand this. [Take] this glass on the table. The glass is form and the table is form. So much of the glass-ness goes off, so much of table-ness [when they break]. ...

The soul ... is nameless because it is formless. It will neither go to heaven nor [to hell] any more than it will enter this glass. It takes the form of the vessel it fills. If it is not in space, either of two things is possible. Either the [soul permeates] space or space is in [it]. You are in space and must have a form. Space limits us, binds us, and makes a form of us. If you are not in space, space is in you. All the heavens and the world are in the person. ...

So it must be with God. God is omnipresent. "Without hands [he grasps] everything; without feet he can move. ... " (Shvetâshvatara Upanishad, III. 19.) He [is] the formless, the deathless, the eternal. The idea of God came. ... He is the Lord of souls, just as my soul is the [lord] of my body. If my soul left the body, the body would not be for a moment. If He left my soul, the soul would not exist. He is the creator of the universe; of everything that dies He is the destroyer. His shadow is death; His shadow is life.

[The ancient Indian philosophers] thought: ... This filthy world is not fit for man's attention. There is nothing in the universe that is [permanent — neither good nor evil]. ...

I told you ... Satan ... did not have much chance [in India]. Why? Because they were very bold in religion. They were not babies. Have you seen that characteristic of children? They are always trying to throw the blame on someone else. Baby minds [are] trying, when they make a mistake, to throw the blame upon someone [else]. On the one hand, we say, "Give me this; give me that." On the other hand, we say, "I did not do this; the devil tempted me. The devil did it." That is the history of mankind, weak mankind. ...

Why is evil? Why is [the world] the filthy, dirty hole? We have made it. Nobody is to blame. We put our hand in the fire. The Lord bless us, [man gets] just what he deserves. Only He is merciful. If we pray to Him, He helps us. He gives Himself to us.

That is their idea. They are [of a] poetic nature. They go crazy over poetry. Their philosophy is poetry. This philosophy is a poem. ... All [high thought] in the Sanskrit is written in poetry. Metaphysics, astronomy — all in poetry.

We are responsible, and how do we come to mischief? [You may say], "I was born poor and miserable. I remember the hard struggle all my life." Philosophers say that you are to blame. You do not mean to say that all this sprang up without any cause whatever? You are a rational being. Your life is not without cause, and you are the cause. You manufacture your own life all the time. ... You make and mould your own life. You are responsible for yourself. Do not lay the blame upon anybody, any Satan. You will only get punished a little more. ...

[A man] is brought up before God, and He says, "Thirty-one stripes for you," ... when comes another man. He says, "Thirty stripes: fifteen for that fellow, and fifteen for the teacher — that awful man who taught him." That is the awful thing in teaching. I do not know what I am going to get. I go all over the world. If I have to get fifteen for each one I have taught!...

We have to come to this idea: "This My Mâyâ is divine."

It is My activity [My] divinity. "[My Maya] is hard to cross, but those that take refuge in me [go beyond maya]." (Gita, VII. 14.) But you find out that it is very difficult to cross this ocean [of Maya by] yourself. You cannot. It is the old question - hen and egg. If you do any work, that work becomes the cause and produces the effect. That effect [again] becomes the cause and produces the effect. And so on. If you push this down, it never stops. Once you set a thing in motion, there is no more stopping. I do some work, good or bad, [and it sets up a chain reaction].... I cannot stop now.

It is impossible for us to get out from this bondage [by ourselves]. It is only possible if there is someone more powerful than this law of causation, and if he takes mercy on us and drags us out.

And we declare that there is such a one - God. There is such a being, all merciful.... If there is a God, then it is possible for me to be saved. How can you be saved by your own will? Do you see the philosophy of the doctrine of salvation by grace? You Western people are wonderfully clever, but when you undertake to explain philosophy, you are so wonderfully complicated. How can you save yourself by work, if by salvation you mean that you will be taken out of all this nature? Salvation means just standing upon God, but if you understand what is meant by salvation, then you are the Self.... You are not nature. You are the only thing outside of souls and gods and nature. These are the external existences, and God [is] interpenetrating both nature and soul.

Therefore, just as my soul is [to] my body, we, as it were, are the bodies of God. God-souls-nature — it is one. The One, because, as I say, I mean the body, soul, and mind. But, we have seen, the law of causation pervades every bit of nature, and once you have got caught you cannot get out. When once you get into the meshes of law, a possible way of escape is not [through work done] by you. You can build hospitals for every fly and flea that ever lived.... All this you may do, but it would never lead to salvation.... [Hospitals] go up and they come down again. [Salvation] is only possible if there is some being whom nature never caught, who is the Ruler of nature. He rules nature instead of being ruled by nature. He wills law instead of being downed by law. ... He exists and he is all merciful. The moment you seek Him [He will save you].

Why has He not taken us out? You do not want Him. You want everything but Him. The moment you want Him, that moment you get Him. We never want Him. We say, "Lord, give me a fine house." We want the house, not Him. "Give me health! Save me from this difficulty!" When a man wants nothing but Him, [he gets Him]. "The same love which wealthy men have for gold and silver and possessions, Lord, may I have the same love for Thee. I want neither earth nor heaven, nor beauty nor learning. I do not want salvation. Let me go to hell again and again. But one thing I want: to love Thee, and for love's sake — not even for heaven."

Whatever man desires, he gets. If you always dream of having a body, [you will get another body]. When this body goes away he wants another, and goes on begetting body after body. Love matter and you become matter. You first become animals. When I see a dog gnawing a bone, I say, "Lord help us!" Love body until you become dogs and cats! Still degenerate, until you become minerals — all body and nothing else....

There are other people, who would have no compromise. The road to salvation is through truth. That was another watchword. ...

[Man began to progress spiritually] when he kicked the devil out. He stood up and took the responsibility of the misery of the world upon his own shoulders. But whenever he looked [at the] past and future and [at the] law of causation, he knelt down and said, "Lord, save me, [thou] who [art] our creator, our father, and dearest friend." That is poetry, but not very good poetry, I think. Why not? It is the painting of the Infinite [no doubt]. You have it in every language how they paint the Infinite. [But] it is the infinite of the senses, of the muscles. ...

"[Him] the sun [does not illumine], nor the moon, nor the stars, [nor] the flash of lightning." (Katha Upanishad, II. ii. 15.) That is another painting of the Infinite, by negative language. ... And the last Infinite is painted in [the] spirituality of the Upanishads. Not only is Vedanta the highest philosophy in the world, but it is the greatest poem....

Mark today, this is the ... difference between the first part of the Vedas and the second. In the first, it is all in [the domain of] sense. But all religions are only [concerned with the] infinite of the external world — nature and nature's God.... [Not so Vedanta]. This is the first light that the human mind throws back [of] all that. No satisfaction [comes] of the infinite [in] space. "[The] Self-exisent [One] has [created] the [senses as turned] ... to the outer world. Those therefore who [seek] outside will never find that [which is within]. There are the few who, wanting to know the truth, turn their eyes inward and in their own souls behold the glory [of the Self]." (Katha Upanishad, II. i. 1.)

It is not the infinite of space, but the real Infinite, beyond space, beyond time.... Such is the world missed by the Occident.... Their minds have been turned to external nature and nature's God. Look within yourself and find the truth that you had [forgotten]. Is it possible for mind to come out of this dream without the help of the gods? Once you start the action, there is no help unless the merciful Father takes us out.

That would not be freedom, [even] at the hands of the merciful God. Slavery is slavery. The chain of gold is quite as bad as the chain of iron. Is there a way out?

You are not bound. No one was ever bound. [The Self] is beyond. It is the all. You are the One; there are no two. God was your own reflection cast upon the screen of Maya. The real God [is the Self]. He [whom man] ignorantly worships is that reflection. [They say that] the Father in heaven is God. Why God? [It is because He is] your own reflection that [He] is God. Do you see how you are seeing God all the time? As you unfold yourself, the reflection grows [clearer].

“Two beautiful birds are there sitting upon the same tree. The one [is] calm, silent, majestic; the one below [the individual self], is eating the fruits, sweet and bitter, and becoming happy and sad. [But when the individual self beholds the worshipful Lord as his own true Self, he grieves no more.]” (Mundaka Upanishad, III. i. 1-2.)

... Do not say “God”. Do not say “Thou”. Say “I”. The language of [dualism] says, “God, Thou, my Father.” The language of [non-dualism] says, “Dearer unto me than I am myself. I would have no name for Thee. The nearest I can use is I....

“God is true. The universe is a dream. Blessed am I that I know this moment that I [have been and] shall be free all eternity; ... that I know that I am worshipping only myself; that no nature, no delusion, had any hold on me. Vanish nature from me, vanish [these] gods; vanish worship; ... vanish superstitions, for I know myself. I am the Infinite. All these — Mrs. So-and-so, Mr. So-and-so, responsibility, happiness, misery — have vanished. I am the Infinite. How can there be death for me, or birth? Whom shall I fear? I am the One. Shall I be afraid of myself? Who is to be afraid of [whom]? I am the one Existence. Nothing else exists. I am everything.”

It is only the question of memory [of your true nature], not salvation by work. Do you get salvation? You are [already] free.

Go on saying, "I am free". Never mind if the next moment delusion comes and says, "I am bound." Dehypnotise the whole thing.

[This truth] is first to be heard. Hear it first. Think on it day and night. Fill the mind [with it] day and night: "I am It. I am the Lord of the universe. Never was there any delusion.... " Meditate upon it with all the strength of the mind till you actually see these walls, houses, everything, melt away — [until] body, everything, vanishes. "I will stand alone. I am the One." Struggle on! "Who cares! We want to be free; [we] do not want any powers. Worlds we renounce; heavens we renounce; hells we renounce. What do I care about all these powers, and this and that! What do I care if the mind is controlled or uncontrolled! Let it run on. What of that! I am not the mind, Let it go on!"

The sun [shines on the just and on the unjust]. Is he touched by the defective [character] of anyone? "I am He. Whatever [my] mind does, I am not touched. The sun is not touched by shining on filthy places, I am Existence."

This is the religion of [non-dual] philosophy. [It is] difficult. Struggle on! Down with all superstitions! Neither teachers nor scriptures nor gods [exist]. Down with temples, with priests, with gods, with incarnations, with God himself! I am all the God that ever existed! There, stand up philosophers! No fear! Speak no more of God and [the] superstition of the world. Truth alone triumphs, and this is true. I am the Infinite.

All religious superstitions are vain imaginations. ... This society, that I see you before me, and [that] I am talking to you — this is all superstition; all must be given up. Just see what it takes to become a philosopher! This is the [path] of [Jnâna-] Yoga, the way through knowledge. The other [paths] are easy, slow, ... but this is pure strength of mind. No weakling [can follow this path of knowledge. You must be able to say:] "I am the Soul, the ever free; [I] never was bound. Time is in me, not I in time. God was born in my mind. God the Father, Father of the universe — he is created by me in my own mind...."

Do you call yourselves philosophers? Show it! Think of this, talk [of] this, and [help] each other in this path, and give up all superstition!

The Sages of India

In speaking of the sages of India, my mind goes back to those periods of which history has no record, and tradition tries in vain to bring the secrets out of the gloom of the past. The sages of India have been almost innumerable, for what has the Hindu nation been doing for thousands of years except producing sages? I will take, therefore, the lives of a few of the most brilliant ones, the epoch-makers, and present them before you, that is to say, my study of them.

In the first place, we have to understand a little about our scriptures. Two ideals of truth are in our scriptures; the one is, what we call the eternal, and the other is not so authoritative, yet binding under particular circumstances, times, and places. The eternal relations which deal with the nature of the soul, and of God, and the relations between souls and God are embodied in what we call the Shrutis, the Vedas. The next set of truths is what we call the Smritis, as embodied in the words of Manu. Yâjnavalkya, and other writers and also in the Purânas, down to the Tantras. The second class of books and teachings is subordinate to the Shrutis, inasmuch as whenever any one of these contradicts anything in the Shrutis, the Shrutis must prevail. This is the law. The idea is that the framework of the destiny and goal of man has been all delineated in the Vedas, the details have been left to be worked out in the Smritis and Puranas. As for general directions, the Shrutis are enough; for spiritual life, nothing more can be said, nothing more can be known. All that is necessary has been known, all the advice that is necessary to lead the soul to perfection has been completed in the Shrutis; the details alone were left out, and these the Smritis have supplied from time to time.

Another peculiarity is that these Shrutis have many sages as the recorders of the truths in them, mostly men, even some women. Very little is known of their personalities, the dates of their birth, and so forth, but their best thoughts, their best discoveries, I should say, are preserved there, embodied in the sacred literature of our country, the Vedas. In the Smritis, on the other hand, personalities are more in evidence. Startling, gigantic, impressive, world-moving persons stand before us, as it were, for the first time, sometimes of more magnitude even than their teachings.

This is a peculiarity which we have to understand — that our religion preaches an Impersonal Personal God. It preaches any amount of impersonal laws plus any amount of personality, but the very fountain-head of our religion is in the Shrutis, the Vedas, which are perfectly impersonal; the persons all come in the Smritis and Puranas — the great Avatâras, Incarnations of God, Prophets, and so forth. And this ought also to be observed that except our religion every other religion in the world depends upon the life or lives of some personal founder or founders. Christianity is built upon the life of Jesus Christ, Mohammedanism upon Mohammed, Buddhism upon Buddha, Jainism upon the Jinas, and so on. It naturally follows that there must be in all these religions a good deal of fight about what they call the historical evidences of these great personalities. If at any time the historical evidences about the existence of these personages in ancient times become weak, the whole building of the religion tumbles down and is broken to pieces. We escaped this fate because our religion is not based upon persons but on principles. That you obey your religion is not because it came through the authority of a sage, no, not even of an Incarnation. Krishna is not the authority of the Vedas, but the Vedas are the authority of Krishna himself. His glory is that he is the greatest preacher of the Vedas that ever existed. So with the other Incarnations; so with all our sages. Our first principle is that all that is necessary for the perfection of man and for attaining unto freedom is there in the Vedas. You cannot find anything new. You cannot go beyond a perfect unity, which is the goal of all knowledge; this has been already reached there, and it is impossible to go beyond the unity. Religious knowledge became complete when Tat Twam Asi (Thou art That) was discovered, and that was in the Vedas. What remained was the guidance of people from time to time according to different times and places, according to different circumstances and environments; people had to be guided along the old, old path, and for this these great teachers came, these great sages. Nothing can bear out more clearly this position than the celebrated saying of Shri Krishna in the Gitâ: "Whenever virtue subsides and irreligion prevails, I create Myself for the protection of the good; for the destruction of all immorality I am coming from time to time." This is the idea in India.

What follows? That on the one hand, there are these eternal principles which stand upon their own foundations without depending on any reasoning even, much less on the authority of sages however great, of Incarnations however brilliant they may have been. We may remark that as this is the unique position in India, our claim is that the Vedanta only can be the universal religion, that it is already the existing universal religion in the world, because it teaches principles and not persons. No religion built upon a person can be taken up as a type by all the races of mankind. In our own country we find that there have been so many grand characters; in even a small city many persons are taken up as types by the different minds in that one city. How is it possible that one person as Mohammed or Buddha or Christ, can be taken up as the one type for the whole world, nay, that the whole of morality, ethics, spirituality, and religion can be true only from the sanction of that one person, and one person alone? Now, the Vedantic religion does not require any such personal authority. Its sanction is the eternal nature of man, its ethics are based upon the eternal spiritual solidarity of man, already existing, already attained and not to be attained. On the other hand, from the very earliest times, our sages have been feeling conscious of this fact that the vast majority of mankind require a personality. They must have a Personal God in some form or other. The very Buddha who declared against the existence of a Personal God had not died fifty years before his disciples manufactured a Personal God out of him. The Personal God is necessary, and at the same time we know that instead of and better than vain imaginations of a Personal God, which in ninety-nine cases out of a hundred are unworthy of human worship we have in this world, living and walking in our midst, living Gods, now and then. These are more worthy of worship than any imaginary God, any creation of our imagination, that is to say, any idea of God which we can form. Shri Krishna is much greater than any idea of

God you or I can have. Buddha is a much higher idea, a more living and idolised idea, than the ideal you or I can conceive of in our minds; and therefore it is that they always command the worship of mankind even to the exclusion of all imaginary deities.

This our sages knew, and, therefore, left it open to all Indian people to worship such great Personages, such Incarnations. Nay, the greatest of these Incarnations goes further: "Wherever an extraordinary spiritual power is manifested by external man, know that I am there, it is from Me that that manifestation comes." That leaves the door open for the Hindu to worship the Incarnations of all the countries in the world. The Hindu can worship any sage and any saint from any country whatsoever, and as a fact we know that we go and worship many times in the churches of the Christians, and many, many times in the Mohammedan mosques, and that is good. Why not? Ours, as I have said, is the universal religion. It is inclusive enough, it is broad enough to include all the ideals. All the ideals of religion that already exist in the world can be immediately included, and we can patiently wait for all the ideals that are to come in the future to be taken in the same fashion, embraced in the infinite arms of the religion of the Vedanta.

This, more or less, is our position with regard to the great sages, the Incarnations of God. There are also secondary characters. We find the word Rishi again and again mentioned in the Vedas, and it has become a common word at the present time. The Rishi is the great authority. We have to understand that idea. The definition is that the Rishi is the Mantra-drashtâ, the seer of thought. What is the proof of religion? — this was asked in very ancient times. There is no proof in the senses was the declaration.

— "From whence words reflect back with thought without reaching the goal."

— "There the eyes cannot reach, neither can speech, nor the mind" — that has been the declaration for ages and ages. Nature outside cannot give us any answer as to the existence of the soul, the existence of God, the eternal life, the goal of man, and all that. This mind is continually changing, always in a state of flux; it is finite, it is broken into pieces. How can nature tell of the Infinite, the Unchangeable, the Unbroken, the Indivisible, the Eternal? It never can. And whenever mankind has striven to get an answer from dull dead matter, history shows how disastrous the results have been. How comes, then, the knowledge which the Vedas declare? It comes through being a Rishi. This knowledge is not in the senses; but are the senses the be-all and the end-all of the human being? Who dare say that the senses are the all-in-all of man? Even in our lives, in the life of every one of us here, there come moments of calmness, perhaps, when we see before us the death of one we loved, when some shock comes to us, or when extreme blessedness comes to us. Many other occasions there are when the mind, as it were, becomes calm, feels for the moment its real nature; and a glimpse of the Infinite beyond, where words cannot reach nor the mind go, is revealed to us. This happens in ordinary life, but it has to be heightened, practiced, perfected. Men found out ages ago that the soul is not bound or limited by the senses, no, not even by consciousness. We have to understand that this consciousness is only the name of one link in the infinite chain. Being is not identical with consciousness, but consciousness is only one part of Being. Beyond consciousness is where the bold search lies. Consciousness is bound by the senses. Beyond that, beyond the senses, men must go in order to arrive at truths of the spiritual world, and there are even now persons who succeed in going beyond the bounds of the senses. These are called Rishis, because they come face to face with spiritual truths.

The proof, therefore, of the Vedas is just the same as the proof of this table before me, Pratyaksha, direct perception. This I see with the senses, and the truths of spirituality we also see in a superconscious state of the human soul. This Rishi-state is not limited by time or place, by sex or race. Vâtsyâyana boldly declares that this Rishihood is the common property of the descendants of the sage, of the Aryan, of the non-Aryan, of even the Mlechchha. This is the sageship of the Vedas, and constantly we ought to remember this ideal of religion in India, which I wish other nations of the world would also remember and learn, so that there may be less fight and less quarrel. Religion is not in books, nor in theories, nor in dogmas, nor in talking, not even in reasoning. It is being and becoming. Ay, my friends, until each one of you has become a Rishi and come face to face with spiritual facts, religious life has not begun for you. Until the superconscious opens for you, religion is mere talk, it is nothing but preparation. You are talking second- hand, third-hand, and here applies that beautiful saying of Buddha when he had a discussion with some Brahmins. They came discussing about the nature of Brahman, and the great sage asked, "Have you seen Brahman?" "No, said the Brahmin; "Or your father?" "No, neither has he"; "Or your grandfather?" "I don't think even he saw Him." "My friend, how can you discuss about a person whom your father and grandfather never saw, and try to put each other down?" That is what the whole world is doing. Let us say in the language of the Vedanta, "This Atman is not to be reached by too much talk, no, not even by the highest intellect, no, not even by the study of the Vedas themselves."

Let us speak to all the nations of the world in the language of the Vedas: Vain are your fights and your quarrels; have you seen God whom you want to preach? If you have not seen, vain is your preaching; you do not know what you say; and if you have seen God, you will not quarrel, your very face will shine. An ancient sage of the Upanishads sent his son out to learn about Brahman, and the child came back, and the father asked, "what have you learnt?" The child replied he had learnt so many sciences. But the father said, "That is nothing, go back." And the son went back, and when he returned again the father asked the same question, and the same answer came from the child. Once more he had to go back. And the next time he came, his whole face was shining; and his father stood up and declared, "Ay, today, my child, your face shines like a knower of Brahman." When you have known God, your very face will be changed, your voice will be changed, your whole appearance will he changed. You will be a blessing to mankind; none will be able to resist the Rishi. This is the Rishihood, the ideal in our religion. The rest, all these talks and reasonings and philosophies and dualisms and monisms, and even the Vedas themselves are but preparations, secondary things. The other is primary. The Vedas, grammar, astronomy, etc., all these are secondary; that is supreme knowledge which makes us realise the Unchangeable One. Those who realised are the sages whom we find in the Vedas; and we understand how this Rishi is the name of a type, of a class, which every one of us, as true Hindus,

is expected to become at some period of our life, and becoming which, to the Hindu, means salvation. Not belief in doctrines, not going to thousands of temples, nor bathing in all the rivers in the world, but becoming the Rishi, the Mantra-drashta — that is freedom, that is salvation.

Coming down to later times, there have been great world-moving sages, great Incarnations of whom there have been many; and according to the Bhâgavata , they also are infinite in number, and those that are worshipped most in India are Râma and Krishna. Rama, the ancient idol of the heroic ages, the embodiment of truth, of morality, the ideal son, the ideal husband, the ideal father, and above all, the ideal king, this Rama has been presented before us by the great sage Vâlmiki. No language can be purer, none chaster, none more beautiful and at the same time simpler than the language in which the great poet has depicted the life of Rama. And what to speak of Sitâ? You may exhaust the literature of the world that is past, and I may assure you that you will have to exhaust the literature of the world of the future, before finding another Sita. Sita is unique; that character was depicted once and for all. There may have been several Ramas, perhaps, but never more than one Sita! She is the very type of the true Indian woman, for all the Indian ideals of a perfected woman have grown out of that one life of Sita; and here she stands these thousands of years, commanding the worship of every man, woman, and child throughout the length and breadth of the land of Âryâvarta. There she will always be, this glorious Sita, purer than purity itself, all patience, and all suffering. She who suffered that life of suffering without a murmur, she the ever-chaste and ever-pure wife, she the ideal of the people, the ideal of the gods, the great Sita, our national God she must always remain. And every one of us knows her too well to require much delineation. All our mythology may vanish, even our Vedas may depart, and our Sanskrit language may vanish for ever, but so long as there will be five Hindus living here, even if only speaking the most vulgar patois, there will be the story of Sita present. Mark my words: Sita has gone into the very vitals of our race. She is there in the blood of every Hindu man and woman; we are all children of Sita. Any attempt to modernise our women, if it tries to take our women away from that ideal of Sita, is immediately a failure, as we see every day. The women of India must grow and develop in the footprints of Sita, and that is the only way.

The next is He who is worshipped in various forms, the favourite ideal of men as well as of women, the ideal of children, as well as of grown-up men. I mean He whom the writer of the Bhagavata was not content to call an Incarnation but says, "The other Incarnations were but parts of the Lord. He, Krishna, was the Lord Himself." And it is not strange that such adjectives are applied to him when we marvel at the many-sidedness of his character. He was the most wonderful Sannyasin, and the most wonderful householder in one; he had the most wonderful amount of Rajas, power, and was at the same time living in the midst of the most wonderful renunciation. Krishna can never he understood until you have studied the Gita, for he was the embodiment of his own teaching. Every one of these Incarnations came as a living illustration of what they came to preach. Krishna, the preacher of the Gita, was all his life the embodiment of that Song Celestial; he was the great illustration of non-attachment. He gives up his throne and never cares for it. He, the leader of India, at whose word kings come down from their thrones, never wants to be a king. He is the simple Krishna, ever the same Krishna who played with the Gopis. Ah, that most marvellous passage of his life, the most difficult to understand, and which none ought to attempt to understand until he has become perfectly chaste and pure, that most marvellous expansion of love, allegorised and expressed in that beautiful play at Vrindâban, which none can understand but he who has become mad with love, drunk deep of the cup of love! Who can understand the throes of the lore of the Gopis — the very ideal of love, love that wants nothing, love that even does not care for heaven, love that does not care for anything in this world or the world to come? And here, my friends, through this love of the Gopis has been found the only solution of the conflict between the Personal and the Impersonal God. We know how the Personal God is the highest point of human life; we know that it is philosophical to believe in an Impersonal God immanent in the universe, of whom everything is but a manifestation. At the same time our souls hanker after something concrete, something which we want to grasp, at whose feet we can pour out our soul, and so on. The Personal God is therefore the highest conception of human nature. Yet reason stands aghast at such an idea. It is the same old, old question which you find discussed in the Brahma-Sutras , which you find Draupadi discussing with Yudhishthira in the forest: If there is a Personal God, all-merciful, all-powerful, why is the hell of an earth here, why did He create this? — He must be a partial God. There was no solution, and the only solution that can be found is what you read about the love of the Gopis. They hated every adjective that was applied to Krishna; they did not care to know that he was the Lord of creation, they did not care to know that he was almighty, they did not care to know that he was omnipotent, and so forth. The only thing they understood was that he was infinite Love, that was all. The Gopis understood Krishna only as the Krishna of Vrindaban. He, the leader of the hosts, the King of kings, to them was the shepherd, and the shepherd for ever. "I do not want wealth, nor many people, nor do I want learning; no, not even do I want to go to heaven. Let one be born again and again, but Lord, grant me this, that I may have love for Thee, and that for love's sake." A great landmark in the history of religion is here, the ideal of love for love's sake, work for work's sake, duty for duty's sake, and it for the first time fell from the lips of the greatest of Incarnations, Krishna, and for the first time in the history of humanity, upon the soil of India. The religions of fear and of temptations were gone for ever, and in spite of the fear of hell and temptation of enjoyment in heaven, came the grandest of ideals, love for love's sake, duty for duty's sake, work for work's sake.

And what a love! I have told you just now that it is very difficult to understand the love of the Gopis. There are not wanting fools, even in the midst of us, who cannot understand the marvellous significance of that most marvellous of all episodes. There are, let me repeat, impure fools, even born of our blood, who try to shrink from that as if from something impure. To them I have only to say, first make yourselves pure; and you must remember that he who tells the history of the love of the Gopis is none else but Shuka Deva. The historian who records this marvellous love of the Gopis is one who was born pure, the eternally pure Shuka, the son of Vyâsa. So long as there its selfishness in the heart, so long is love of God impossible; it is nothing but shopkeeping: "I give you something; O Lord, you give me something in return"; and says the Lord, "If you do not do this, I will take good care of you when you die. I will roast you all the rest of your lives. perhaps", and so on. So long as such ideas are in the brain, how can one understand the mad throes of the Gopis' love? "O for one, one kiss of those lips! One who has been kissed by Thee, his thirst for Thee increases for ever, all sorrows vanish, and he forgets love for everything else but for Thee and Thee alone." Ay, forget first the love for gold, and name and fame, and for this little trumpery world of ours. Then, only then, you will understand the love of the Gopis, too holy to be attempted without giving up everything, too sacred to be understood until the soul has become perfectly pure. People with ideas of sex, and of money, and of fame, bubbling up every minute in the heart, daring to criticise and understand the love of the Gopis! That is the very essence of the Krishna Incarnation. Even the Gita, the great philosophy itself, does not compare with that madness, for in the Gita the disciple is taught slowly how to walk towards the goal, but here is the madness of enjoyment, the drunkenness of love, where disciples and teachers and teachings and books and all these things have become one; even the ideas of fear, and God, and heaven — everything has been thrown away. What remains is the madness of love. It is forgetfulness of everything, and the lover sees nothing in the world except that Krishna and Krishna alone, when the face of every being becomes a Krishna, when his own face looks like Krishna, when his own soul has become tinged with the Krishna colour. That was the great Krishna!

Do not waste your time upon little details. Take up the framework, the essence of the life. There may be many historical discrepancies, there may be interpolations in the life of Krishna. All these things may be true; but, at the same time, there must have been a basis, a foundation for this new and tremendous departure. Taking the life of any other sage or prophet, we find that that prophet is only the evolution of what had gone before him, we find that that prophet is only preaching the ideas that had been scattered about his own country even in his own times. Great doubts may exist even as to whether that prophet existed or not. But here, I challenge any one to show whether these things, these ideals — work for work's sake, love for love's sake, duty for duty's sake, were not original ideas with Krishna, and as such, there must have been someone with whom these ideas originated. They could not have been borrowed from anybody else. They were not floating about in the atmosphere when Krishna was born. But the Lord Krishna was the first preacher of this; his disciple Vyasa took it up and preached it unto mankind. This is the highest idea to picture. The highest thing we can get out of him is Gopijanavallabha, the Beloved of the Gopis of Vrindaban. When that madness comes in your brain, when you understand the blessed Gopis, then you will understand what love is. When the whole world will vanish, when all other considerations will have died out, when you will become pure-hearted with no other aim, not even the search after truth, then and then alone will come to you the madness of that love, the strength and the power of that infinite love which the Gopis had, that love for love's sake. That is the goal. When you have got that, you have got everything.

To come down to the lower stratum — Krishna, the preacher of the Gita. Ay, there is an attempt in India now which is like putting the cart before the horse. Many of our people think that Krishna as the lover of the Gopis is something rather uncanny, and the Europeans do not like it much. Dr. So-and-so does not like it. Certainly then, the Gopis have to go! Without the sanction of Europeans how can Krishna live? He cannot! In the Mahabharata there is no mention of the Gopis except in one or two places, and those not very remarkable places. In the prayer of Draupadi there is mention of a Vrindaban life, and in the speech of Shishupâla there is again mention of this Vrindaban. All these are interpolations! What the Europeans do not want: must be thrown off. They are interpolations, the mention of the Gopis and of Krishna too! Well, with these men, steeped in commercialism, where even the ideal of religion has become commercial, they are all trying to go to heaven by doing something here; the bania wants compound interest, wants to lay by something here and enjoy it there. Certainly the Gopis have no place in such a system of thought. From that ideal lover we come down to the lower stratum of Krishna, the preacher of the Gita. Than the Gita no better commentary on the Vedas has been written or can be written. The essence of the Shrutis, or of the Upanishads, is hard to be understood, seeing that there are so many commentators, each one trying to interpret in his own way. Then the Lord Himself comes, He who is the inspirer of the Shrutis, to show us the meaning of them, as the preacher of the Gita, and today India wants nothing better, the world wants nothing better than that method of interpretation. It is a wonder that subsequent interpreters of the scriptures, even commenting upon the Gita, many times could not catch the meaning, many times could not catch the drift. For what do you find in the Gita, and what in modern commentators? One nondualistic commentator takes up an Upanishad; there are so many dualistic passages, and he twists and tortures them into some meaning, and wants to bring them all into a meaning of his own. If a dualistic commentator comes, there are so many nondualistic texts which he begins to torture, to bring them all round to dualistic meaning. But you find in the Gita there is no attempt at torturing any

one of them. They are all right, says the Lord; for slowly and gradually the human soul rises up and up, step after step, from the gross to the fine, from the fine to the finer, until it reaches the Absolute, the goal. That is what is in the Gita. Even the Karma Kanda is taken up, and it is shown that although it cannot give salvation direct; but only indirectly, yet that is also valid; images are valid indirectly; ceremonies, forms, everything is valid only with one condition, purity of the heart. For worship is valid and leads to the goal if the heart is pure and the heart is sincere; and all these various modes of worship are necessary, else why should they be there? Religions and sects are not the work of hypocrites and wicked people who invented all these to get a little money, as some of our modern men want to think. However reasonable that explanation may seem, it is not true, and they were not invented that way at all. They are the outcome of the necessity of the human soul. They are all here to satisfy the hankering and thirst of different classes of human minds, and you need not preach against them. The day when that necessity will cease, they will vanish along with the cessation of that necessity; and so long as that necessity remains, they must be there in spite of your preaching, in spite of your criticism. You may bring the sword or the gun into play, you may deluge the world with human blood, but so long as there is a necessity for idols, they must remain. These forms, and all the various steps in religion will remain, and we understand from the Lord Shri Krishna why they should.

A rather sadder chapter of India's history comes now. In the Gita we already hear the distant sound of the conflicts of sects, and the Lord comes in the middle to harmonise them all; He, the great preacher of harmony, the greatest teacher of harmony, Lord Shri Krishna. He says, "In Me they are all strung like pearls upon a thread." We already hear the distant sounds, the murmurs of the conflict, and possibly there was a period of harmony and calmness, when it broke out anew, not only on religious grounds, but roost possibly on caste grounds — the fight between the two powerful factors in our community, the kings and the priests. And from the topmost crest of the wave that deluged India for nearly a thousand years, we see another glorious figure, and that was our Gautama Shâkyamuni. You all know about his teachings and preachings. We worship him as God incarnate, the greatest, the boldest preacher of morality that the world ever saw, the greatest Karma-Yogi; as disciple of himself, as it were, the same Krishna came to show how to make his theories practical. There came once again the same voice that in the Gita preached, "Even the least bit done of this religion saves from great fear". "Women, or Vaishyas, or even Shudras, all reach the highest goal." Breaking the bondages of all, the chains of all, declaring liberty to all to reach the highest goal, come the words of the Gita, rolls like thunder the mighty voice of Krishna: "Even in this life they have conquered relativity, whose minds are firmly fixed upon the sameness, for God is pure and the same to all, therefore such are said to be living in God." "Thus seeing the same Lord equally present everywhere, the sage does not injure the Self by the self, and thus reaches the highest goal." As it were to give a living example of this preaching, as it were to make at least one part of it practical, the preacher himself came in another form, and this was Shakyamuni, the preacher to the poor and the miserable, he who rejected even the language of the gods to speak in the language of the people, so that he might reach the hearts of the people, he who gave up a throne to live with beggars, and the poor, and the downcast, he who pressed the Pariah to his breast like a second Rama.

You all know about his great work, his grand character. But the work had one great defect, and for that we are suffering even today. No blame attaches to the Lord. He is pure and glorious, but unfortunately such high ideals could not be well assimilated by the different uncivilised and uncultured races of mankind who flocked within the fold of the Aryans. These races, with varieties of superstition and hideous worship, rushed within the fold of the Aryans and for a time appeared as if they had become civilised, but before a century had passed they brought out their snakes, their ghosts, and all the other things their ancestors used to worship, and thus the whole of India became one degraded mass of superstition. The earlier Buddhists in their rage against the killing of animals had denounced the sacrifices of the Vedas; and these sacrifices used to be held in every house. There was a fire burning, and that was all the paraphernalia of worship. These sacrifices were obliterated, and in their place came gorgeous temples, gorgeous ceremonies, and gorgeous priests, and all that you see in India in modern times. I smile when I read books written by some modern people who ought to have known better, that the Buddha was the destroyer of Brahminical idolatry. Little do they know that Buddhism created Brahminism and idolatry in India.

There was a book written a year or two ago by a Russian gentleman, who claimed to have found out a very curious life of Jesus Christ, and in one part of the book he says that Christ went to the temple of Jagannath to study with the Brahmins, but became disgusted with their exclusiveness and their idols, and so he went to the Lamas of Tibet instead, became perfect, and went home. To any man who knows anything about Indian history, that very statement proves that the whole thing was a fraud, because the temple of Jagannath is an old Buddhistic temple. We took this and others over and re-Hinduised them. We shall have to do many things like that yet. That is Jagannath, and there was not one Brahmin there then, and yet we are told that Jesus Christ came to study with the Brahmins there. So says our great Russian archaeologist.

Thus, in spite of the preaching of mercy to animals, in spite of the sublime ethical religion, in spite of the hairsplitting discussions about the existence or non-existence of a permanent soul, the whole building of Buddhism tumbled down piecemeal; and the ruin was simply hideous. I have neither the time nor the inclination to describe to you the hideousness that came in the wake of Buddhism. The most hideous ceremonies, the most horrible, the most obscene books that human hands ever wrote or the human brain ever conceived, the most bestial forms that ever passed under the name of religion, have all been the creation of degraded Buddhism.

But India has to live, and the spirit of the Lords descended again. He who declared, "I will come whenever virtue subsides", came again, and this time the manifestation was in the South, and up rose that young Brahmin of whom it has been declared that at the age of sixteen he had completed all his writings; the marvellous boy Shankaracharya arose. The writings of this boy of sixteen are the wonders of the modern world, and so was the boy. He wanted to bring back the Indian world to its pristine purity, but think of the amount of the task before him. I have told you a few points about the state of things that existed in India. All these horrors that you are trying to reform are the outcome of that reign of degradation. The Tartars and the Baluchis and all the hideous races of mankind came to India and became Buddhists, and assimilated with us, and brought their national customs, and the whole of our national life became a huge page of the most horrible and the most bestial customs. That was the inheritance which that boy got from the Buddhists, and from that time to this, the whole work in India is a reconquest of this Buddhistic degradation by the Vedanta. It is still going on, it is not yet finished. Shankara came, a great philosopher, and showed that the real essence of Buddhism and that of the Vedanta are not very different, but that the disciples did not understand the Master and have degraded themselves, denied the existence of the soul and of God, and have become atheists. That was what Shankara showed, and all the Buddhists began to come back to the old religion. But then they had become accustomed to all these forms; what could be done?

Then came the brilliant Râmânuja. Shankara, with his great intellect, I am afraid, had not as great a heart. Ramanuja's heart was greater. He felt for the downtrodden, he sympathised with them. He took up the ceremonies, the accretions that had gathered, made them pure so far as they could be, and instituted new ceremonies, new methods of worship, for the people who absolutely required them. At the same time he opened the door to the highest; spiritual worship from the Brahmin to the Pariah. That was Ramanuja's work. That work rolled on, invaded the North, was taken up by some great leaders there; but that was much later, during the Mohammedan rule; and the brightest of these prophets of comparatively modern times in the North was Chaitanya.

You may mark one characteristic since the time of Ramanuja — the opening of the door of spirituality to every one. That has been the watchword of all prophets succeeding Ramanuja, as it had been the watchword of all the prophets before Shankara. I do not know why Shankara should be represented as rather exclusive; I do not find anything in his writings which is exclusive. As in the case of the declarations of the Lord Buddha, this exclusiveness that has been attributed to Shankara's teachings is most possibly not due to his teachings, but to the incapacity of his disciples. This one great Northern sage, Chaitanya, represented the mad love of the Gopis. Himself a Brahmin, born of one of the most rationalistic families of the day, himself a professor of logic fighting and gaining a word-victory — for, this he had learnt from his childhood as the highest ideal of life and yet through the mercy of some sage the whole life of that man became changed; he gave up his fight, his quarrels, his professorship of logic and became one of the greatest teachers of Bhakti the world has ever known

— mad Chaitanya. His Bhakti rolled over the whole land of Bengal, bringing solace to every one. His love knew no bounds. The saint or the sinner, the Hindu or the Mohammedan, the pure or the impure, the prostitute, the streetwalker — all had a share in his love, all had a share in his mercy: and even to the present day, although greatly degenerated, as everything does become in time, his sect is the refuge of the poor, of the downtrodden, of the outcast, of the weak, of those who have been rejected by all society. But at the same time I must remark for truth's sake that we find this: In the philosophic sects we find wonderful liberalisms. There is not a man who follows Shankara who will say that all the different sects of India are really different. At the same time he was a tremendous upholder of exclusiveness as regards caste. But with every Vaishnavite preacher we find a wonderful liberalism as to the teaching of caste questions, but exclusiveness as regards religious questions.

The one had a great head, the other a large heart, and the time was ripe for one to be born, the embodiment of both this head and heart; the time was ripe for one to be born who in one body would have the brilliant intellect of Shankara and the wonderfully expansive, infinite heart of Chaitanya; one who would see in every sect the same spirit working, the same God; one who would see God in every being, one whose heart would weep for the poor, for the weak, for the outcast, for the downtrodden, for every one in this world, inside India or outside India; and at the same time whose grand brilliant intellect would conceive of such noble thoughts as would harmonise all conflicting sects, not only in India but outside of India, and bring a marvellous harmony, the universal religion of head and heart into existence. Such a man was born, and I had the good fortune to sit at his feet for years. The time was ripe, it was necessary that such a man should be born, and he came; and the most wonderful part of it was that his life's work was just near a city which was full of Western thought, a city which had run mad after these occidental ideas, a city which had become more Europeanised than any other city in India. There he lived, without any book-learning whatsoever; this great intellect never learnt even to write his own name, [9] but the most graduates of our university found in him an intellectual giant. He was a strange man, this Shri Ramakrishna Paramahamsa. It is a long, long story, and I have no time to tell anything about him tonight. Let me now only mention the great Shri Ramakrishna, the fulfilment of the Indian sages, the sage for the time, one whose teaching is just now, in the present time, most beneficial. And mark the divine power working behind the man. The son of a poor priest, born in an out-of-the-way village, unknown and unthought of, today is worshipped literally by thousands in Europe and America, and tomorrow will be worshipped by thousands more. Who knows the plans of the Lord!

Now, my brothers, if you do not see the hand, the finger of Providence, it is because you are blind, born blind indeed. If time comes, and another opportunity, I will speak to you more fully about him. Only let me say now that if I have told you one word of truth, it was his and his alone, and if I have told you many things which were not true, which were not correct, which were not beneficial to the human race, they were all mine, and on me is the responsibility.

Practical Religion: Breathing and Meditation

This article was recorded by Ida Ansell in shorthand. As, however, Swamiji's speed was too great for her in her early days, dots are put in the articles to indicate the omissions, while the words within square brackets are added by way of linking up the disconnected parts.

(Delivered in San Francisco, April 5, 1900)

Everyone's idea of practical religion is according to his theory of practicality and the standpoint he starts from. There is work. There is the system of worship. There is knowledge.

The philosopher thinks ... the difference between bondage and freedom is only caused by knowledge and ignorance. To him, knowledge is the goal, and his practicality is gaining that knowledge.... The worshipper's practical religion is the power of love and devotion. The worker's practical religion consists in doing good works. And so, as in every other thing, we are always trying to ignore the standard of another, trying to bind the whole world to our standard.

Doing good to his fellow-beings is the practical religion of the man full of love. If men do not help to build hospitals, he thinks that they have no religion at all. But there is no reason why everyone should do that. The philosopher, in the same way, may denounce every man who does not have knowledge. People may build twenty thousand hospitals, and the philosopher declares they are but ... the beasts of burden of the gods. The worshipper has his own idea and standard: Men who cannot love God are no good, whatever work they do. The [Yogi believes in] psychic [control and] the conquest of [internal] nature. "How much have you gained towards that? How much control over your senses, over your body?"— that is all the Yogi asks. And, as we said, each one judges the others by his own standard. Men may have given millions of dollars and fed rats and cats, as some do in India. They say that men can take care of themselves, but the poor animals cannot. That is their idea. But to the Yogi the goal is conquest of [internal] nature, and he judges man by that standard....

We are always talking [about] practical religion. But it must be practical in our sense. Especially [so] in the Western countries. The Protestants' ideal is good works. They do not care much for devotion and philosophy. They think there is not much in it. "What is your knowledge!" [they say]. "Man has to do something!" ... A little humanitarianism! The churches rail day and night against callous agnosticism. Yet they seem to be veering rapidly towards just that. Callous slaves! Religion of utility! That is the spirit just now. And that is why some Buddhists have become so popular in the West. People do not know whether there is a God or not, whether there is a soul or not. [They think :] This world is full of misery. Try to help this world.

The Yoga doctrine, which we are having our lecture on, is not from that standpoint. [It teaches that] there is the soul, and inside this soul is all power. It is already there, and if we can master this body, all the power will be unfolded. All knowledge is in the soul. Why are people struggling? To lessen the misery.... All unhappiness is caused by our not having mastery over the body.... We are all putting the cart before the horse.... Take the system of work, for instance. We are trying to do good by ... comforting the poor. We do not get to the cause which created the misery. It is like taking a bucket to empty out the ocean, and more [water] comes all the time. The Yogi sees that this is nonsense. [He says that] the way out of misery is to know the cause of misery first.... We try to do the good we can. What for? If there is an incurable disease, why should we struggle and take care of ourselves? If the utilitarians say: "Do not bother about soul and God!" what is that to the Yogi and what is it to the world? The world does not derive any good [from such an attitude]. More and more misery is going on all the time....

The Yogi says you are to go to the root of all this. Why is there misery in the world? He answers: "It is all our own foolishness, not having proper mastery of our own bodies. That is all." He advises the means by which this misery can be [overcome]. If you can thus get mastery of your body, all the misery of the world will vanish. Every hospital is praying that more and more sick people will come there. Every time you think of doing some charity, you think there is some beggar to take your charity. If you say, "O Lord, let the world be full of charitable people!" — you mean, let the world be full of beggars also. Let the world be full of good works - let the world be full of misery. This is out-and-out slavishness!

.. The Yogi says, religion is practical if you know first why misery exists. All the misery in the world is in the senses. Is there any ailment in the sun, moon, and stars? The same fire that cooks your meal burns the child. Is it the fault of the fire? Blessed be the fire! Blessed be this electricity! It gives light.... Where can you lay the blame? Not on the elements. The world is neither good nor bad; the world is the world. The fire is the fire. If you burn your finger in it, you are a fool. If you [cook your meal and with it satisfy your hunger,] you are a wise man. That is all the difference. Circumstances can never be good or bad. Only the individual man can be good or bad. What is meant by the world being good or bad? Misery and happiness can only belong to the sensuous individual man.

The Yogis say that nature is the enjoyed; the soul is the enjoyer. All misery and happiness — where is it? In the senses. It is the touch of the senses that causes pleasure and pain, heat and cold. If we can control the senses and order what they shall feel — not let them order us about as they are doing now — if they can obey our commands, become our servants, the problem is solved at once. We are bound by the senses; they play upon us, make fools of us all the time.

Here is a bad odour. It will bring me unhappiness as soon as it touches my nose. I am the slave of my nose. If I am not its slave, I do not care. A man curses me. His curses enter my ears and are retained in my mind and body. If I am the master, I shall say: "Let these things go; they are nothing to me. I am not miserable. I do not bother." This is the outright, pure, simple, clear-cut truth.

The other problem to be solved is — is it practical? Can man attain to the power of mastery of the body? ... Yoga says it is practical .... Supposing it is not — suppose there are doubts in your mind. You have got to try it. There is no other way out....

You may do good works all the time. All the same, you will be the slave of your senses, you will be miserable and unhappy. You may study the philosophy of every religion. Men in this country carry loads and loads of books on their backs. They are mere scholars, slaves of the senses, and therefore happy and unhappy. They read two thousand books, and that is all right; but as soon as a little misery comes, they are worried, anxious.... You call yourselves men! You stand up ... and build hospitals. You are fools!

What is the difference between men and animals? ... "Food and [sleep], procreation of the species, and fear exist in common with the animals. There is one difference: Man can control all these and become God, the master." Animals cannot do it. Animals can do charitable work. Ants do it. Dogs do it. What is the difference then? Men can be masters of themselves. They can resist the reaction to anything.... The animal cannot resist anything. He is held ... by the string of nature everywhere. That is all the distinction. One is the master of nature, the other the slave of nature. What is nature? The five senses....

[The conquest of internal nature] is the only way out, according to Yoga.... The thirst for God is religion.... Good works and all that [merely] make the mind a little quiet. To practice this — to be perfect — all depends upon our past. I have been studying [Yoga] all my life and have made very little progress yet. But I have got enough [result] to believe that this is the only true way. The day will come when I will be master of myself. If not in this life, [in another life]. I will struggle and never let go. Nothing is lost. If I die this moment, all my past struggles [will come to my help]. Have you not seen what makes the difference between one man and another? It is their past. The past habits make one man a genius and another man a fool. You may have the power of the past and can succeed in five minutes. None can predict the moment of time. We all have to attain [perfection] some time or other.

The greater part of the practical lessons which the Yogi gives us is in the mind, the power of concentration and meditation.... We have become so materialistic. When we think of ourselves, we find only the body. The body has become the ideal, nothing else. Therefore a little physical help is necessary....

First, to sit in the posture In which you can sit still for a long time. All the nerve currents which are working pass along the spine. The spine is not intended to support the weight of the body. Therefore the posture must be such that the weight of the body is not on the spine. Let it be free from all pressure.

There are some other preliminary things. There is the great question of food and exercise....

The food must be simple and taken several times [a day] instead of once or twice. Never get very hungry. “He who eats too much cannot be a Yogi. He who fasts too much cannot be a Yogi. He who sleeps too much cannot be a Yogi, nor he who keeps awake too much.” (Gita, VI. 16.) He who does not do any work and he who works too hard cannot succeed. Proper food, proper exercise, proper sleep, proper wakefulness — these are necessary for any success.

What the proper food is, what kind, we have to determine ourselves. Nobody can determine that [for us]. As a general practice, we have to shun exciting food.... We do not know how to vary our diet with our occupation. We always forget that it is the food out of which we manufacture everything we have. So the amount and kind of energy that we want, the food must determine....

Violent exercises are not all necessary.... If you want to be muscular, Yoga is not for you. You have to manufacture a finer organism than you have now. Violent exercises are positively hurtful.... Live amongst those who do not take too much exercise. If you do not take violent exercise, you will live longer. You do not want to burn out your lamp in muscles! People who work with their brains are the longest-lived people.... Do not burn the lamp quickly. Let it burn slowly and gently.... Every anxiety, every violent exercise — physical and mental — [means] you are burning the lamp.

The proper diet means, generally, simply do not eat highly spiced foods. There are three sorts of mind, says the Yogi, according to the elements of nature. One is the dull mind, which covers the luminosity of the soul. Then there is that which makes people active, and lastly, that which makes them calm and peaceful.

Now there are persons born with the tendency to sleep all the time. Their taste will be towards that type of food which is rotting — crawling cheese. They will eat cheese that fairly jumps off the table. It is a natural tendency with them.

Then active people. Their taste is for everything hot and pungent, strong alcohol....

Sâttvika people are very thoughtful, quiet, and patient. They take food in small quantities, and never anything bad.

I am always asked the question: "Shall I give up meat?" My Master said, "Why should you give up anything? It will give you up." Do not give up anything in nature. Make it so hot for nature that she will give you up. There will come a time when you cannot possibly eat meat. The very sight of it will disgust you. There will come a time when many things you are struggling to give up will be distasteful, positively loathsome.

Then there are various sorts of breathing exercises. One consists of three parts: the drawing in of the breath, the holding of the breath — stopping still without breathing — and throwing the breath out. [Some breathing exercises] are rather difficult, and some of the complicated ones are attended with great danger if done without proper diet. I would not advise you to go through any one of these except the very simple ones.

Take a deep breath and fill the lungs. Slowly throw the breath out. Take it through one nostril and fill the lungs, and throw it out slowly through the other nostril. Some of us do not breathe deeply enough. Others cannot fill the lungs enough. These breathings will correct that very much. Half an hour in the morning and half an hour in the evening will make you another person. This sort of breathing is never dangerous. The other exercises should be practiced very slowly. And measure your strength. If ten minutes are a drain, only take five.

The Yogi is expected to keep his own body well. These various breathing exercises are a great help in regulating the different parts of the body. All the different parts are inundated with breath. It is through breath that we gain control of them all. Disharmony in parts of the body is controlled by more flow of the nerve currents towards them. The Yogi ought to be able to tell when in any part pain is caused by less vitality or more. He has to equalise that....

Another condition [for success in Yoga] is chastity. It is the corner-stone of all practice. Married or unmarried — perfect chastity. It is a long subject, of course, but I want to tell you: Public discussions of this subject are not to the taste of this country. These Western countries are full of the most degraded beings in the shape of teachers who teach men and women that if they are chaste they will be hurt. How do they gather all this? ... People come to me — thousands come every year — with this one question. Someone has told them that if they are chaste and pure they will be hurt physically.... How do these teachers know it? Have they been chaste? Those unchaste, impure fools, lustful creatures, want to drag the whole world down to their [level]! ...

Nothing is gained except by sacrifice.... The holiest function of our human consciousness, the noblest, do not make it unclean! Do not degrade it to the level of the brutes.... Make yourselves decent men! ... Be chaste and pure! ... There is no other way. Did Christ find any other way? ... If you can conserve and use the energy properly, it leads you to God. Inverted, it is hell itself ....

It is much easier to do anything upon the external plane, but the greatest conqueror in the world finds himself a mere child when he tries to control his own mind. This is the world he has to conquer — the greater and more difficult world to conquer. Do not despair! Awake, arise, and stop not until the goal is reached!...

Work and Its Secret

One of the greatest lessons I have learnt in my life is to pay as much attention to the means of work as to its end. He was a great man from whom I learnt it, and his own life was a practical demonstration of this great principle I have been always learning great lessons from that one principle, and it appears to me that all the secret of success is there; to pay as much attention to the means as to the end.

Our great defect in life is that we are so much drawn to the ideal, the goal is so much more enchanting, so much more alluring, so much bigger in our mental horizon, that we lose sight of the details altogether.

But whenever failure comes, if we analyse it critically, in ninety-nine per cent of cases we shall find that it was because we did not pay attention to the means. Proper attention to the finishing, strengthening, of the means is what we need. With the means all right, the end must come. We forget that it is the cause that produces the effect; the effect cannot come by itself; and unless the causes are exact, proper, and powerful, the effect will not be produced. Once the ideal is chosen and the means determined, we may almost let go the ideal, because we are sure it will be there, when the means are perfected. When the cause is there, there is no more difficulty about the effect, the effect is bound to come. If we take care of the cause, the effect will take care of itself. The realization of the ideal is the effect. The means are the cause: attention to the means, therefore, is the great secret of life. We also read this in the Gita and learn that we have to work, constantly work with all our power; to put our whole mind in the work, whatever it be, that we are doing. At the same time, we must not be attached. That is to say, we must not be drawn away from the work by anything else; still, we must be able to quit the work whenever we like.

If we examine our own lives, we find that the greatest cause of sorrow is this: we take up something, and put our whole energy on it — perhaps it is a failure and yet we cannot give it up. We know that it is hurting us, that any further clinging to it is simply bringing misery on us; still, we cannot tear ourselves away from it. The bee came to sip the honey, but its feet stuck to the honey-pot and it could not get away. Again and again, we are finding ourselves in that state. That is the whole secret of existence. Why are we here? We came here to sip the honey, and we find our hands and feet sticking to it. We are caught, though we came to catch. We came to enjoy; we are being enjoyed. We came to rule; we are being ruled. We came to work; we are being worked. All the time, we find that. And this comes into every detail of our life. We are being worked upon by other minds, and we are always struggling to work on other minds. We want to enjoy the pleasures of life; and they eat into our vitals. We want to get everything from nature, but we find in the long run that nature takes everything from us — depletes us, and casts us aside.

Had it not been for this, life would have been all sunshine. Never mind! With all its failures and successes, with all its joys and sorrows, it can be one succession of sunshine, if only we are not caught.

That is the one cause of misery: we are attached, we are being caught. Therefore says the Gita: Work constantly; work, but be not attached; be not caught. Reserve unto yourself the power of detaching yourself from everything, however beloved, however much the soul might yearn for it, however great the pangs of misery you feel if you were going to leave it; still, reserve the power of leaving it whenever you want. The weak have no place here, in this life or in any other life. Weakness leads to slavery. Weakness leads to all kinds of misery, physical and mental. Weakness is death. There are hundreds of thousands of microbes surrounding us, but they cannot harm us unless we become weak, until the body is ready and predisposed to receive them. There may be a million microbes of misery, floating about us. Never mind! They dare not approach us, they have no power to get a hold on us, until the mind is weakened. This is the great fact: strength is life, weakness is death. Strength is felicity, life eternal, immortal; weakness is constant strain and misery: weakness is death.

Attachment is the source of all our pleasures now. We are attached to our friends, to our relatives; we are attached to our intellectual and spiritual works; we are attached to external objects, so that we get pleasure from them. What, again, brings misery but this very attachment? We have to detach ourselves to earn joy. If only we had power to detach ourselves at will, there would not be any misery. That man alone will be able to get the best of nature, who, having the power of attaching himself to a thing with all his energy, has also the power to detach himself when he should do so. The difficulty is that there must be as much power of attachment as that of detachment. There are men who are never attracted by anything. They can never love, they are hard-hearted and apathetic; they escape most of the miseries of life. But the wall never feels misery, the wall never loves, is never hurt; but it is the wall, after all. Surely it is better to be attached and caught, than to be a wall. Therefore the man who never loves, who is hard and stony, escaping most of the miseries of life, escapes also its joys. We do not want that. That is weakness, that is death. That soul has not been awakened that never feels weakness, never feels misery. That is a callous state. We do not want that.

At the same time, we not only want this mighty power of love, this mighty power of attachment, the power of throwing our whole soul upon a single object, losing ourselves and letting ourselves be annihilated, as it were, for other souls — which is the power of the gods — but we want to be higher even than the gods. The perfect man can put his whole soul upon that one point of love, yet he is unattached. How comes this? There is another secret to learn.

The beggar is never happy. The beggar only gets a dole with pity and scorn behind it, at least with the thought behind that the beggar is a low object. He never really enjoys what he gets.

We are all beggars. Whatever we do, we want a return. We are all traders. We are traders in life, we are traders in virtue, we are traders in religion. And alas! we are also traders in love.

If you come to trade, if it is a question of give-and-take, if it is a question of buy-and-sell, abide by the laws of buying and selling. There is a bad time and there is a good time; there is a rise and a fall in prices: always you expect the blow to come. It is like looking at the mirrors Your face is reflected: you make a grimace — there is one in the mirror; if you laugh, the mirror laughs. This is buying and selling, giving and taking.

We get caught. How? Not by what we give, but by what we expect. We get misery in return for our love; not from the fact that we love, but from the fact that we want love in return. There is no misery where there is no want. Desire, want, is the father of all misery. Desires are bound by the laws of success and failure. Desires must bring misery.

The great secret of true success, of true happiness, then, is this: the man who asks for no return, the perfectly unselfish man, is the most successful. It seems to be a paradox. Do we not know that every man who is unselfish in life gets cheated, gets hurt? Apparently, yes. "Christ was unselfish, and yet he was crucified." True, but we know that his unselfishness is the reason, the cause of a great victory — the crowning of millions upon millions of lives with the blessings of true success.

Ask nothing; want nothing in return. Give what you have to give; it will come back to you — but do not think of that now, it will come back multiplied a thousandfold — but the attention must not be on that. Yet have the power to give: give, and there it ends. Learn that the whole of life is giving, that nature will force you to give. So, give willingly. Sooner or later you will have to give up. You come into life to accumulate. With clenched hands, you want to take. But nature puts a hand on your throat and makes your hands open. Whether you will it or not, you have to give. The moment you say, "I will not", the blow comes; you are hurt. None is there but will be compelled, in the long run, to give up everything. And the more one struggles against this law, the more miserable one feels. It is because we dare not give, because we are not resigned enough to accede to this grand demand of nature, that we are miserable. The forest is gone, but we get heat in return. The sun is taking up water from the ocean, to return it in showers. You are a machine for taking and giving: you take, in order to give. Ask, therefore, nothing in return; but the more you give, the more will come to you. The quicker you can empty the air out of this room, the quicker it will be filled up by the external air; and if you close all the doors and every aperture, that which is within will remain, but that which is outside will never come in, and that which is within will stagnate, degenerate, and become poisoned. A river is continually emptying itself into the ocean and is continually filling up again. Bar not the exit into the ocean. The moment you do that, death seizes you.

Be, therefore, not a beggar; be unattached This is the most terrible task of life! You do not calculate the dangers on the path. Even by intellectually recognising the difficulties, we really do not know them until we feel them. From a distance we may get a general view of a park: well, what of that? We feel and really know it when we are in it. Even if our every attempt is a failure, and we bleed and are torn asunder, yet, through all this, we have to preserve our heart — we must assert our Godhead in the midst of all these difficulties. Nature wants us to react, to return blow for blow, cheating for cheating, lie for lie, to hit back with all our might. Then it requires a superdivine power not to hit back, to keep control, to be unattached.

Every day we renew our determination to be unattached. We cast our eyes back and look at the past objects of our love and attachment, and feel how every one of them made us miserable. We went down into the depths of despondency because of our "love"! We found ourselves mere slaves in the hands of others, we were dragged down and down! And we make a fresh determination: "Henceforth, I will be master of myself; henceforth, I will have control over myself." But the time comes, and the same story once more! Again the soul is caught and cannot get out. The bird is in a net, struggling and fluttering. This is our life.

I know the difficulties. Tremendous they are, and ninety per cent of us become discouraged and lose heart, and in our turn, often become pessimists and cease to believe in sincerity, love, and all that is grand and noble. So, we find men who in the freshness of their lives have been forgiving, kind, simple, and guileless, become in old age lying masks of men. Their minds are a mass of intricacy.

There may be a good deal of external policy, possibly. They are not hot-headed, they do not speak, but it would be better for them to do so; their hearts are dead and, therefore, they do not speak. They do not curse, not become angry; but it would be better for them to be able to be angry, a thousand times better, to be able to curse. They cannot. There is death in the heart, for cold hands have seized upon it, and it can no more act, even to utter a curse, even to use a harsh word.

All this we have to avoid: therefore I say, we require superdivine power. Superhuman power is not strong enough. Superdivine strength is the only way, the one way out. By it alone we can pass through all these intricacies, through these showers of miseries, unscathed. We may be cut to pieces, torn asunder, yet our hearts must grow nobler and nobler all the time.

It is very difficult, but we can overcome the difficulty by constant practice. We must learn that nothing can happen to us, unless we make ourselves susceptible to it. I have just said, no disease can come to me until the body is ready; it does not depend alone on the germs, but upon a certain predisposition which is already in the body. We get only that for which we are fitted. Let us give up our pride and understand this, that never is misery undeserved. There never has been a blow undeserved: there never has been an evil for which I did not pave the way with my own hands. We ought to know that. Analyse yourselves and you will find that every blow you have received, came to you because you prepared yourselves for it. You did half, and the external world did the other half: that is how the blow came. That will sober us down. At the same time, from this very analysis will come a note of hope, and the note of hope is: "I have no control of the external world, but that which is in me and nearer unto me, my own world, is in my control. If the two together are required to make a failure, if the two together are necessary to give me a blow, I will not contribute the one which is in my keeping; and how then can the blow come? If I get real control of myself, the blow will never come."

We are all the time, from our childhood, trying to lay the blame upon something outside ourselves. We are always standing up to set right other people, and not ourselves. If we are miserable, we say, "Oh, the world is a devil's world." We curse others and say, "What infatuated fools!" But why should we be in such a world, if we really are so good? If this is a devil's world, we must be devils also; why else should we be here? "Oh, the people of the world are so selfish!" True enough; but why should we be found in that company, if we be better? Just think of that.

We only get what we deserve. It is a lie when we say, the world is bad and we are good. It can never be so. It is a terrible lie we tell ourselves.

This is the first lesson to learn: be determined not to curse anything outside, not to lay the blame upon any one outside, but be a man, stand up, lay the blame on yourself. You will find, that is always true. Get hold of yourself.

Is it not a shame that at one moment we talk so much of our manhood, of our being gods — that we know everything, we can do everything, we are blameless, spotless, the most unselfish people in the world; and at the next moment a little stone hurts us, a little anger from a little Jack wounds us — any fool in the street makes "these gods" miserable! Should this be so if we are such gods? Is it true that the world is to blame? Could God, who is the purest and the noblest of souls, be made miserable by any of our tricks? If you are so unselfish, you are like God. What world can hurt you? You would go through the seventh hell unscathed, untouched. But the very fact that you complain and want to lay the blame upon the external world shows that you feel the external world — the very fact that you feel shows that you are not what you claim to be. You only make your offence greater by heaping misery upon misery, by imagining that the external world is hurting you, and crying out, "Oh, this devil's world! This man hurts me; that man hurts me! " and so forth. It is adding lies to misery.

We are to take care of ourselves — that much we can do — and give up attending to others for a time. Let us perfect the means; the end will take care of itself. For the world can be good and pure, only if our lives are good and pure. It is an effect, and we are the means. Therefore, let us purify ourselves. Let us make ourselves perfect.

The Power of the Mind

The cause becomes the effect. The cause is not one thing and the effect something else that exists as a result. The effect is always the cause worked out. Always, the cause becomes the effect. The popular idea is that the effect is the result of the operation of a cause which is something independent and aloof from the effect. al his is not so. The effect is always the cause worked out into another condition.

The universe is really homogeneous. Heterogeneity is only in appearance. There seem to be different substances, different powers, etc. throughout nature. But take two different substances, say a piece of glass and a piece of wood, grind them up together fine enough, reduce them till there is nothing more to reduce, and the substance remaining appears homogeneous. All substances in the last analysis are one. Homogeneity is the substance, the reality; heterogeneity is the appearance of many things as though they were mans' substances. The One is homogeneity; the appearance of the One as many is heterogeneity.

Hearing, seeing, or tasting, etc. is the mind in different states of action.

The atmosphere of a room may be hypnotised so that everybody who enters it will see all sorts of things — men and objects flying through the air.

Everybody is hypnotised already. The work of attaining freedom, of realising one's real nature, consists in de-hypnotisation.

One thing to be remembered is that we are not gaining powers at all. We have them already. The whole process of growth is de-hypnotisation.

The purer the mind, the easier it is to control. Purity of the mind must be insisted upon if you would control it. Do not think covetously about mere mental powers. Let them go. One who seeks the powers of the mind succumbs to them. Almost all who desire powers become ensnared by them.

Perfect morality is the all in all of complete control over mind. The man who is perfectly moral has nothing more to do; he is free. The man who is perfectly moral cannot possibly hurt anything or anybody. Non-injuring has to be attained by him who would be free. No one is more powerful than he who has attained perfect non-injuring. No one could fight, no one could quarrel, in his presence. Yes, his very presence, and nothing else, means peace, means love wherever he may be. Nobody could be angry or fight in his presence. Even the animals, ferocious animals, would be peaceful before him.

I once knew a Yogi, a very old man, who lived in a hole in the ground all by himself. (Pavhâri Bâbâ of Ghazipur. (See Vol. IV. Sketch of the Life of Pavhari Baba)) All he had was a pan or two to cook his meals in. He ate very little, and wore scarcely anything, and spent most of his time meditating.

With him all people were alike. He had attained to non-injuring. What he saw in everything, in every person, in every animal, was the Soul, the Lord of the Universe. With him, every person and every animal was "my Lord". He never addressed any person or animal in any other way. Well, one day a thief came his way and stole one of his pans. He saw him and ran after him. The chase was a long one. At last the thief from exhaustion had to stop, and the Yogi, running up to him, fell on his knees before him and said, "My Lord, you do me a great honour to come my way. Do me the honour to accept the other pan. It is also yours." This old man is dead now. He was full of love for everything in the world. He would have died for an ant. Wild animals instinctively knew this old man to be their friend. Snakes and ferocious animals would go into his hole and sleep with him. They all loved him and never fought in his presence.

Never talk about the faults of others, no matter how bad they may be. Nothing is ever gained by that. You never help one by talking about his fault; you do him an injury, and injure yourself as well.

All regulations in eating, practicing, etc., are all right so long as they are complementary to a spiritual aspiration but they are not ends in themselves; they are only helps.

Never quarrel about religion. All quarrels and disputations concerning religion simply show that spirituality is not present. Religious quarrels are always over the husks. When purity, when spirituality goes, leaving the soul dry, quarrels begin, and not before.

ADDRESSES ON BHAKTI-YOGA

THE PREPARATION

The best definition given of Bhakti-Yoga is perhaps embodied in the verse: "May that love undying which the non-discriminating have for the fleeting objects of the senses never leave this heart of mine — of me who seek after Thee!" We see what a strong love men, who do not know any better, have for sense-objects, for money, dress, their wives, children, friends, and possessions. What a tremendous clinging they have to all these things! So in the above prayer the sage says, "I will have that attachment, that tremendous clinging, only to Thee." This love, when given to God, is called Bhakti. Bhakti is not destructive; it teaches us that no one of the faculties we have has been given in vain, that through them is the natural way to come to liberation. Bhakti does not kill out our tendencies, it does not go against nature, but only gives it a higher and more powerful direction. How naturally we love objects of the senses! We cannot but do so, because they are so real to us. We do not ordinarily see anything real about higher things, but when a man has seen something real beyond the senses, beyond the universe of senses, the idea is that he can have a strong attachment, only it should be transferred to the object beyond the senses, which is God. And when the same kind of love that has before been given to sense-objects is given to God, it is called Bhakti. According to the sage Râmânuja, the following are the preparations for getting that intense love.

The first is Viveka. It is a very curious thing, especially to people of the West. It means, according to Ramanuja, "discrimination of food". Food contains all the energies that go to make up the forces of our body and mind; it has been transferred, and conserved, and given new directions in my body, but my body and mind have nothing essentially different from the food that I ate. Just as the force and matter we find in the material world become body and mind in us, so, essentially, the difference between body and mind and the food we eat is only in manifestation. It being so, that out of the material particles of our food we construct the instrument of thought, and that from the finer forces lodged in these particles we manufacture thought itself, it naturally follows, that both this thought and the instrument will be modified by the food we take. There are certain kinds of food that produce a certain change in the mind; we see it every day. There are other sorts which produce a change in the body, and in the long run have a tremendous effect on the mind. It is a great thing to learn; a good deal of the misery we suffer is occasioned by the food we take. You find that after a heavy and indigestible meal it is very hard to control the mind; it is running, running all the time. There are certain foods which are exciting; if you eat such food, you find that you cannot control the mind. It is obvious that after drinking a large quantity of wine, or other alcoholic beverage, a man finds that his mind would not be controlled; it runs away from his control.

According to Ramanuja, there are three things in food we must avoid. First, there is Jâti, the nature, or species of the food, that must be considered. All exciting food should be avoided, as meat, for instance; this should not be taken because it is by its very nature impure. We can get it only by taking the life of another. We get pleasure for a moment, and another creature has to give up its life to give us that pleasure. Not only so, but we demoralise other human beings. It would be rather better if every man who eats meat killed the animal himself; but, instead of doing so, society gets a class of persons to do that business for them, for doing which, it hates them. In England no butcher can serve on a jury, the idea being that he is cruel by nature. Who makes him cruel? Society. If we did not eat beef and mutton, there would be no butchers. Eating meat is only allowable for people who do very hard work, and who are not going to be Bhaktas; but if you are going to be Bhaktas, you should avoid meat. Also, all exciting foods, such as onions, garlic, and all evil-smelling food, as "sauerkraut". Any food that has been standing for days, till its condition is changed, any food whose natural juices have been almost dried ups any food that is malodorous, should be avoided.

The next thing that is to be considered as regards food is still more intricate to Western minds — it is what is called Âshraya, i.e. the person from whom it comes This is rather a mysterious theory of the Hindus. The idea is that each man has a certain aura round him, and whatever thing he touches, a part of his character, as it were, his influence, is left on it. It is supposed that a man's character emanates from him, as it were, like a physical force, and whatever he touches is affected by it. So we must take care who touches our food when it is cooked; a wicked or immoral person must not touch it. One who wants to be a Bhakta must not dine with people whom he knows to be very wicked, because their infection will come through the food.

The other form of purity to be observed is Nimitta, or instruments. Dirt and dust must not be in food. Food should not be brought from the market and placed on the table unwashed. We must be careful also about the saliva and other secretions. The lips ought never, for instance, to be touched with the fingers. The mucous membrane is the most delicate part of the body, and all tendencies are conveyed very easily by the saliva. Its contact, therefore, is to be regarded as not only offensive, but dangerous. Again, we must not eat food, half of which has been eaten by someone else. When these things are avoided in food, it becomes pure; pure food brings a pure mind, and in a pure mind is a constant memory of God.

Let me tell you the same thing as explained by another commentator, Shankarâchârya, who takes quite another view. This word for food, in Sanskrit, is derived from the root, meaning to gather. Âhâra means "gathered in". What is his explanation? He says, the passage that when food is pure the mind will become pure really means that lest we become subject to the senses we should avoid the following: First as to attachment; we must not be extremely attached to anything excepting God. See everything, do everything, but be not attached. As soon as extreme attachment comes, a man loses himself, he is no more master of himself, he is a slave. If a woman is tremendously attached to a man, she becomes a slave to that man. There is no use in being a slave. There are higher things in this world than becoming a slave to a human being. Love and do good to everybody, but do not become a slave. In the first place, attachment degenerates us, individually, and in the second place, makes us extremely selfish. Owing to this failing, we want to injure others to do good to those we love. A good many of the wicked deeds done in this world are really done through attachment to certain persons. So all attachment excepting that for good works should be avoided; but love should be given to everybody. Then as to jealousy. There should be no jealousy in regard to objects of the senses; jealousy is the root of all evil, and a most difficult thing to conquer. Next, delusion. We always take one thing for another, and act upon that, with the result that we bring misery upon ourselves. We take the bad for the good. Anything that titillates our nerves for a moment we think; as the highest good, and plunge into it immediately, but find, when it is too late, that it has given us a tremendous blow. Every day, we run into this error, and we often continue in it all our lives. When the senses, without being extremely attached, without jealousy, or without delusion, work in the world, such work or collection of impressions is called pure food, according to Shankaracharya. When pure food is taken, the mind is able to take in objects and think about them without attachment, jealousy or delusion; then the mind becomes pure, and then there is constant memory of God in that mind.

It is quite natural for one to say that Shankara's meaning is the best, but I wish to add that one should not neglect Ramanuja's interpretation either. It is only when you take care of the real material food that the rest will come. It is very true that mind is the master, but very few of us are not bound by the senses. We are all controlled by matter; and as long as we are so controlled, we must take material aids; and then, when we have become strong, we can eat or drink anything we like. We have to follow Ramanuja in taking care about food and drink; at the same time we must also take care about our mental food. It is very easy to take care about material food, but mental work must go along with it; then gradually our spiritual self will become stronger and stronger, and the physical self less assertive. Then will food hurt you no more. The great danger is that every man wants to jump at the highest ideal, but jumping is not the way. That ends only in a fall. We are bound down here, and we have to break our chains slowly. This is called Viveka, discrimination.

The next is called Vimoka, freedom from desires. He who wants to love God must get rid of extreme desires, desire nothing except God. This world is good so far as it helps one to go to the higher world. The objects of the senses are good so far as they help us to attain higher objects. We always forget that this world is a means to an end, and not an end itself. If this were the end we should be immortal here in our physical body; we should never die. But we see people every moment dying around us, and yet, foolishly, we think we shall never die; and from that conviction we come to think that this life is the goal. That is the case with ninety-nine per cent of us. This notion should be given up at once. This world is good so far as it is a means to perfect ourselves; and as soon as it has ceased to be so, it is evil. So wife, husband, children, money and learning, are good so long as they help us forward; but as soon as they cease to do that, they are nothing but evil. If the wife help us to attain God, she is a good wife; so with a husband or a child. If money help a man to do good to others, it is of some value; but if not, it is simply a mass of evil, and the sooner it is got rid of, the better.

The next is Abhyâsa, practice. The mind should always go towards God. No other things have any right to withhold it. It should continuously think of God, though this is a very hard task; yet it can be done by persistent practice. What we are now is the result of our past practice. Again, practice makes us what we shall be. So practice the other way; one sort of turning round has brought us this way, turn the other way and get out of it as soon as you can. Thinking of the senses has brought us down here — to cry one moment, to rejoice the next, to be at the mercy of every breeze, slave to everything. This is shameful, and yet we call ourselves spirits. Go the other way, think of God; let the mind not think of any physical or mental enjoyment, but of God alone. When it tries to think of anything else, give it a good blow, so that it may turn round and think of God. As oil poured from one vessel to another falls in an unbroken line, as chimes coming from a distance fall upon the ear as one continuous sound, so should the mind flow towards God in one continuous stream. We should not only impose this practice on the mind, but the senses too should be employed. Instead of hearing foolish things, we must hear about God; instead of talking foolish words, we must talk of God. Instead of reading foolish books, we must read good ones which tell of God.

The greatest aid to this practice of keeping God in memory is, perhaps, music. The Lord says to Nârada, the great teacher of Bhakti, "I do not live in heaven, nor do I live in the heart of the Yogi, but where My devotees sing My praise, there am I". Music has such tremendous power over the human mind; it brings it to concentration in a moment. You will find the dull, ignorant, low, brute-like human beings, who never steady their mind for a moment at other times, when they hear attractive music, immediately become charmed and concentrated. Even the minds of animals, such as dogs, lions, cats, and serpents, become charmed with music.

The next is Kriyâ, work — doing good to others. The memory of God will not come to the selfish man. The more we come out and do good to others, the more our hearts will be purified, and God will be in them. According to our scriptures, there are five sorts of work, called the fivefold sacrifice. First, study. A man must study every day something holy and good. Second, worship of God, angels, or saints, as it may be. Third, our duty to our forefathers. Fourth, our duty to human beings. Man has no right to live in a house himself, until he builds for the poor also, or for anybody who needs it. The householder's house should be open to everybody that is poor and suffering; then he is a real householder. If he builds a house only for himself and his wife to enjoy, he will never be a lover of God. No man has the right to cook food only for himself; it is for others, and he should have what remains. It is a common practice in India that when the season's produce first comes into the market, such as strawberries or mangoes, a man buys some of them and gives to the poor. Then he eats of them; and it is a very good example to follow in this country. This training will make a man unselfish, and at the same time, be an excellent object-lesson to his wife and children. The Hebrews in olden times used to give the first fruits to God. The first of everything should go to the poor; we have only a right to what remains. The poor are God's representatives; anyone that suffers is His representative. Without giving, he who eats and enjoys eating, enjoys sin. Fifth, our duty to the lower animals. It is diabolical to say that all animals are created for men to be killed and used in any way man likes. It is the devil's gospel, not God's. Think how diabolical it is to cut them up to see whether a nerve quivers or not, in a certain part of the body. I am glad that in our country such things are not countenanced by the Hindus, whatever encouragement they may get from the foreign government they are under. One portion of the food cooked in a household belongs to the animals also. They should be given food every day; there ought to be hospitals in every city in this country for poor, lame, or blind horses, cows, dogs, and cats, where they should be fed and taken care of.

Then there is Kalyâna, purity, which comprises the following: Satya, truthfulness. He who is true, unto him the God of truth comes. Thought, word, and deed should be perfectly true. Next Ârjava, straightforwardness, rectitude. The word means, to be simple, no crookedness in the heart, no double-dealing. Even if it is a little harsh, go straightforward, and not crookedly. Dayâ, pity, compassion. Ahimsâ, not injuring any being by thought, word, or deed. Dâna, charity. There is no higher virtue than charity. The lowest man is he whose hand draws in, in receiving; and he is the highest man whose hand goes out in giving. The hand was made to give always. Give the last bit of bread you have even if you are starving. You will be free in a moment if you starve yourself to death by giving to another. Immediately you will be perfect, you will become God. People who have children are bound already. They cannot give away. They want to enjoy their children, and they must pay for it. Are there not enough children in the world? It is only selfishness which says, "I'll have a child for myself".

The next is Anavasâda — not desponding, cheerfulness. Despondency is not religion, whatever else it may be. By being pleasant always and smiling, it takes you nearer to God, nearer than any prayer. How can those minds that are gloomy and dull love? If they talk of love, it is false; they want to hurt others. Think of the fanatics; they make the longest faces, and all their religion is to fight against others in word and act. Think of what they have done in the past, and of what they would do now if they were given a free hand. They would deluge the whole world in blood tomorrow if it would bring them power. By worshipping power and making long faces, they lose every bit of love from their hearts. So the man who always feels miserable will never come to God. It is not religion, it is diabolism to say, "I am so miserable." Every man has his own burden to bear. If you are miserable, try to be happy, try to conquer it.

God is not to be reached by the weak. Never be weak. You must be strong; you have infinite strength within you. How else will you conquer anything? How else will you come to God? At the same time you must avoid excessive merriment, Uddharsha, as it is called. A mind in that state never becomes calm; it becomes fickle. Excessive merriment will always be followed by sorrow. Tears and laughter are near kin. People so often run from one extreme to the other. Let the mind be cheerful, but calm. Never let it run into excesses, because every excess will be followed by a reaction.

These, according to Ramanuja, are the preparations for Bhakti.

THE FIRST STEPS

The philosophers who wrote on Bhakti defined it as extreme love for God. Why a man should love God is the question to be solved; and until we understand that, we shall not be able to grasp the subject at all. There are two entirely different ideals of life. A man of any country who has any religion knows that he is a body and a spirit also. But there is a great deal of difference as to the goal of human life.

In Western countries, as a rule, people lay more stress on the body aspect of man; those philosophers who wrote on Bhakti in India laid stress on the spiritual side of man; and this difference seems to be typical of the Oriental and Occidental nations. It is so even in common language. In England, when speaking of death it is said, a man gave up his ghost; in India, a man gave up his body. The one idea is that man is a body and has a soul; the other that man is a soul and has a body. More intricate problems arise out of this. It naturally follows that the ideal which holds that man is a body and has a soul lays all the stress on the body. If you ask why man lives, you will be told it is to enjoy the senses, to enjoy possessions and wealth. He cannot dream of anything beyond even if he is told of it; his idea of a future life would be a continuation of this enjoyment. He is very sorry that it cannot continue all the time here, but he has to depart; and he thinks that somehow or other he will go to some place where the same thing will be renewed. He will have the same enjoyments, the same senses, only heightened and strengthened. He wants to worship God, because God is the means to attain this end. The goal of his life is enjoyment of sense-objects, and he comes to know there is a Being who can give him a very long lease of these enjoyments, and that is why he worships God.

On the other hand the Indian idea is that God is the goal of life; there is nothing beyond God, and the sense-enjoyments are simply something through which we are passing now in the hope of getting better things. Not only so; it would be disastrous and terrible if man had nothing but sense-enjoyments. In our everyday life we find that the less the sense-enjoyments, the higher the life of the man. Look at the dog when he eats. No man ever ate with the same satisfaction. Observe the pig giving grunts of satisfaction as he eats; it is his heaven, and if the greatest archangel came and looked on, the pig would not even notice him. His whole existence is in his eating. No man was ever born who could eat that way. Think of the power of hearing in the lower animals, the power of seeing; all their senses are highly developed. Their enjoyment of the senses is extreme; they become simply mad with delight and pleasure. And the lower the man also, the more delight he finds in the senses. As he gets higher, the goal becomes reason and love. In proportion as these faculties develop, he loses the power of enjoying the senses.

For illustration's sake, if we take for granted that a certain amount of power is given to man, and that that can be spent either on the body, or the mind, or the spirit, then all the powers spent on any one of these leaves just so much less to be expended on the others. The ignorant or savage races have much stronger sensual faculties than the civilised races, and this is, in fact, one of the lessons we learn from history that as a nation becomes civilised the nerve organisation becomes finer, and they become physically weaker. Civilise a savage race, and you will find the same thing; another barbarian race comes up and conquers it. It is nearly always the barbarian race that conquers. We see then that if we desire only to have sense-enjoyments all the time, we degrade ourselves to the brute state. A man does not know what he is asking for when he says, he wants to go to a place where his sense-enjoyments will be intensified; that he can only have by going down to the brutes.

So with men desiring a heaven full of sense-pleasures. They are like swine wallowing in the mire of the senses, unable to see anything beyond. This sense-enjoyment is what they want, and the loss of it is the loss of heaven to them. These can never be Bhaktas in the highest sense of the word; they can never be true lovers of God. At the same time, though this lower ideal be followed for a time, it will also in course of time change, each man will find that there is something higher, of which he did not know, and so this clinging to life and to things of the senses will gradually die away. When I was a little boy at school, I had a fight with another schoolfellow about some sweetmeats, and he being the stronger boy snatched them from my hand. I remember the feeling I had; I thought that boy was the most wicked boy ever born, and that as soon as I grew strong enough I would punish him; there was no punishment sufficient for his wickedness. We have both grown up now, and we are fast friends. This world is full of babies to whom eating and drinking, and all these little cakes are everything. They will dream of these cakes, and their idea of future life is where these cakes will be plentiful. Think of the American Indian who believes that his future life will be in a place which is a very good hunting ground. Each one of us has an idea of a heaven just as we want it to be; but in course of time, as we grow older and see higher things, we catch higher glimpses beyond. But let us not dispense with our ideas of future life in the ordinary way of modern times, by not believing in anything — that is destruction. The agnostic who thus destroys everything is mistaken, the Bhakta sees higher. The agnostic does not want to go to heaven, because he has none; while the Bhakta does not want to go to heaven, because he thinks it is child's play. What he wants is God.

What can be a higher end than God? God Himself is the highest goal of man; see Him, enjoy Him. We can never conceive anything higher, because God is perfection. We cannot conceive of any higher enjoyment than that of love, but this word love has different meanings. It does not mean the ordinary selfish love of the world; it is blasphemy to call that love. The love for our children and our wives is mere animal love; that love which is perfectly unselfish is the only love, and that is of God. It is a very difficult thing to attain to. We are passing through all these different loves — love of children, father, mother, and so forth. We slowly exercise the faculty of love; but in the majority of cases we never learn anything from it, we become bound to one step, to one person. In some cases men come out of this bondage. Men are ever running after wives and wealth and fame in this world; sometimes they are hit very hard on the head, and they find out what this world really is. No one in this world can really love anything but God. Man finds out that human love is all hollow. Men cannot love though they talk of it. The wife says she loves her husband and kisses him; but as soon as he dies, the first thing she thinks about is the bank account, and what she shall do the next day. The husband loves the wife; but when she becomes sick and loses her beauty, or becomes haggard, or makes a mistake, he ceases to care for her. All the love of the world is hypocrisy and hollowness.

A finite subject cannot love, nor a finite object be loved. When the object of the love of a man is dying every moment, and his mind also is constantly changing as he grows, what eternal love can you expect to find in the world? There cannot be any real love but in God: why then all these loves? These are mere stages. There is a power behind impelling us forward, we do not know where to seek for the real object, but this love is sending us forward in search of it. Again and again we find out our mistake. We grasp something, and find it slips through our fingers, and then we grasp something else. Thus on and on we go, till at last comes light; we come to God, the only One who loves. His love knows no change and is ever ready to take us in. How long would any of you bear with me if I injured you? He in whose mind is no anger, hatred, or envy, who never loses his balance, dies, or is born, who is he but God? But the path to God is long and difficult, and very few people attain Him. We are all babies struggling. Millions of people make a trade of religion. A few men in a century attain to that love of God, and the whole country becomes blessed and hallowed. When a son of God appears, a whole country becomes blessed. It is true that few such are born in any one century in the whole world, but all should strive to attain that love of God. Who knows but you or I may be the next to attain? Let us struggle therefore.

We say that a wife loves her husband. She thinks that her whole soul is absorbed in him: a baby comes and half of it goes out to the baby, or more. She herself will feel that the same love of husband does not exist now. So with the father. We always find that when more intense objects of love come to us, the previous love slowly vanishes. Children at school think that some of their schoolfellows are the dearest beings that they have in life, or their fathers or mothers are so; then comes the husband or wife, and immediately the old feeling disappears, and the new love becomes uppermost. One star arises, another bigger one comes, and then a still bigger one, and at last the sun comes, and all the lesser lights vanish. That sun is God. The stars are the smaller loves. When that Sun bursts upon him, a man becomes mad what Emerson calls "a God-intoxicated man". Man becomes transfigured into God, everything is merged in that one ocean of love. Ordinary love is mere animal attraction. Otherwise why is the distinction between the sexes? If one kneels before an image, it is dreadful idolatry; but if one kneels before husband or wife, it is quite permissible!

The world presents to us manifold stages of love. We have first to clear the ground. Upon our view of life the whole theory of love will rest. To think that this world is the aim and end of life is brutal and degenerating. Any man who starts in life with that idea degenerates himself He will never rise higher, he will never catch this glimpse from behind, he will always be a slave to the senses. He will struggle for the dollar that will get him a few cakes to eat. Better die than live that life. Slaves of this world, slaves of the senses, let us rouse ourselves; there is something higher than this sense-life. Do you think that man, the Infinite Spirit was born to be a slave to his eyes, his nose, and his ears? There is an Infinite, Omniscient Spirit behind that can do everything, break every bond; and that Spirit we are, and we get that power through love. This is the ideal we must remember. We cannot, of course, get it in a day. We may fancy that we have it, but it is a fancy after all; it is a long, long way off. We must take man where he stands, and help him upwards. Man stands in materialism; you and I are materialists. Our talking about God and Spirit is good; but it is simply the vogue in our society to talk thus: we have learnt it parrot-like and repeat it. So we have to take ourselves where we are as materialists, and must take the help of matter and go on slowly until we become real spiritualists, and feel ourselves spirits, understand the spirit, and find that this world which we call the infinite is but a gross external form of that world which is behind.

But something besides that is necessary. You read in the Sermon on the Mount, "Ask, and it shall be given (to) you; seek, and ye shall find; knock, and it shall be opened unto you." The difficulty is, who seeks, who wants? We all say we know God. One man writes a book to disprove God, another to prove Him. One man thinks it his duty to prove Him all his life; another, to disprove Him, and he goes about to teach man there is no God. What is the use of writing a book either to prove or disprove God? What does it matter to most people whether there is a God or not ? The majority of men work just like a machine with no thought of God and feeling no need of Him. Then one day comes Death and says, "Come." The man says, "Wait a little, I want a little more time. I want to see my son grow a little bigger." But Death says, "Come at once." So it goes on. So goes poor John. What shall we say to poor John? He never found anything in which God was the highest; perhaps he was a pig in the past, and he is much better as a man. But there are some who get a little awakening. Some misery comes, someone whom we love most dies, that upon which we had bent our whole soul, that for which we had cheated the whole world and perhaps our own brother, that vanishes, and a blow comes to us. Perhaps a voice comes in our soul and asks, "What after this?" Sometimes death comes without a blow, but such cases are few. Most of us, when anything slips through our fingers, say, "What next?" How we cling to the senses! You have heard of a drowning man clutching at a straw; a man will clutch at a straw first, and when it fails, he will say someone must help him. Still people must, as the English phrase goes, "sow their wild oats", before they can rise to higher things.

Bhakti is a religion. Religion is not for the many, that is impossible. A sort of knee-drill, standing up and sitting down, may be suited for the many; but religion is for the few. There are in every country only a few hundreds who can be, and will be religious. The others cannot be religious, because they will not be awakened, and they do not want to be. The chief thing is to want God. We want everything except God, because our ordinary wants are supplied by the external world; it is only when our necessities have gone beyond the external world that we want a supply from the internal, from God. So long as our needs are confined within the narrow limits of this physical universe, we cannot have any need for God; it is only when we have become satiated with everything here that we look beyond for a supply. It is only when the need is there that the demand will come. Have done with this child's play of the world as soon as you can, and then you will feel the necessity of something beyond the world, and the first step in religion will come.

There is a form of religion which is fashionable. My friend has much furniture in her parlour; it is the fashion to have a Japanese vase, so she must have one even if it costs a thousand dollars. In the same way she will have a little religion and join a church. Bhakti is not for such. That is not want . Want is that without which we cannot live. We want breath, we want food, we want clothes; without them we cannot live. When a man loves a woman in this world, there are times when he feels that without her he cannot live, although that is a mistake. When a husband dies, the wife thinks she cannot live without him; but she lives all the same. This is the secret of necessity: it is that without which we cannot live; either it must come to us or we die. When the time comes that we feel the same about God, or in other words, we want something beyond this world, something above all material forces, then we may become Bhaktas. What are our little lives when for a moment the cloud passes away, and we get one glimpse from beyond, and for that moment all these lower desires seem like a drop in the ocean? Then the soul grows, and feels the want of God, and must have Him.

The first step is: What do we want? Let us ask ourselves this question every day, do we want God? You may read all the books in the universe, but this love is not to be had by the power of speech, not by the highest intellect, not by the study of various sciences. He who desires God will get Love, unto him God gives Himself. Love is always mutual, reflective. You may hate me, and if I want to love you, you repulse me. But if I persist, in a month or a year you are bound to love me. It is a wellknown psychological phenomenon. As the loving wife thinks of her departed husband, with the same love we must desire the Lord, and then we will find God, and all books and the various sciences would not be able to teach us anything. By reading books we become parrots; no one becomes learned by reading books. If a man reads but one word of love, he indeed becomes learned. So we want first to get that desire.

Let us ask ourselves each day, "Do we want Gods" When we begin to talk religion, and especially when we take a high position and begin to teach others, we must ask ourselves the same question. I find many times that I don't want God, I want bread more. I may go mad if I don't get a piece of bread; many ladies will go mad if they don't get a diamond pin, but they do not have the same desire for God; they do not know the only Reality that is in the universe. There is a proverb in our language — If I want to be a hunter, I'll hunt the rhinoceros; if I want to be a robber, I'll rob the king's treasury. What is the use of robbing beggars or hunting ants? So if you want to love, love God. Who cares for these things of the world? This world is utterly false; all the great teachers of the world found that out; there is no way out of it but through God. He is the goal of our life; all ideas that the world is the goal of life are pernicious. This world and this body have their own value, a secondary value, as a means to an end; but the world should not be the end. Unfortunately, too often we make the world the end and God the means. We find people going to church and saying, "God, give me such and such; God, heal my disease." They want nice healthy bodies; and because they hear that someone will do this work for them, they go and pray to Him. It is better to be an atheist than to have such an idea of religion. As I have told you, this Bhakti is the highest ideal; I don't know whether we shall reach it or not in millions of years to come, but we must make it our highest ideal, make our senses aim at the highest. If we cannot get to the end, we shall at least come nearer to it. We have slowly to work through the world and the senses to reach God.

THE TEACHER OF SPIRITUALITY

Every soul is destined to be perfect, and every being, in the end, will attain to that state. Whatever we are now is the result of whatever we have been or thought in the past; and whatever we shall be in the future will be the result of what we do or think now. But this does not preclude our receiving help from outside; the possibilities of the soul are always quickened by some help from outside, so much so that in the vast majority of cases in the world, help from outside is almost absolutely necessary. Quickening influence comes from outside, and that works upon our own potentialities; and then the growth begins, spiritual life comes, and man becomes holy and perfect in the end. This quickening impulse which comes from outside cannot be received from books; the soul can receive impulse only from another soul, and from nothing else. We may study books all our lives, we may become very intellectual, but in the end we find we have not developed at all spiritually. It does not follow that a high order of intellectual development always shows an equivalent development of the spiritual side of man; on the other hand, we find cases almost every day where the intellect has become very highly developed at the expense of the spirit.

Now in intellectual development we can get much help from books, but in spiritual development, almost nothing. In studying books, sometimes we are deluded into thinking that we are being spiritually helped; but if we analyse ourselves, we shall find that only our intellect has been helped, and not the spirit. That is the reason why almost everyone of us can speak most wonderfully on spiritual subjects, but when the time of action comes, we find ourselves so woefully deficient. It is because books cannot give us that impulse from outside. To quicken the spirit, that impulse must come from another soul.

That soul from which this impulse comes is called the Guru, the teacher; and the soul to which the impulse is conveyed is called the disciple, the student. In order to convey this impulse, in the first place, the soul from which it comes must possess the power of transmitting it, as it were, to another; and in the second place, the object to which it is transmitted must be fit to receive it. The seed must be a living seed, and the field must be ready ploughed; and when both these conditions are fulfilled, a wonderful growth of religion takes place. "The speaker of religion must be wonderful, so must the hearer be"; and when both of these are really wonderful, extraordinary, then alone will splendid spiritual growth come, and not otherwise. These are the real teachers, and these are the real students. Besides these, the others are playing with spirituality — just having a little intellectual struggle, just satisfying a little curiosity — but are standing only on the outward fringe of the horizon of religion. There is some value in that; real thirst for religion may thus be awakened; all comes in course of time. It is a mysterious law of nature that as soon as the field is ready the seed must come, as soon as the soul wants religion, the transmitter of religious force must come. "The seeking sinner meeteth the seeking Saviour." When the power that attracts in the receiving soul is full and ripe, the power which answers to that attraction must come.

But there are great dangers in the way. There is the danger to the receiving soul of mistaking its momentary emotion for real religious yearning. We find that in ourselves. Many times in our lives, somebody dies whom we loved; we receive a blow; for a moment we think that this world is slipping between our fingers, and that we want something higher, and that we are going to be religious. In a few days that wave passes away, and we are left stranded where we were. We ofttimes mistake such impulses for real thirst after religion, but so long as these momentary emotions are thus mistaken, that continuous, real want of the soul will not come, and we shall not find the "transmitter".

So when we complain that we have not got the truth, and that we want it so much, instead of complaining, our first duty ought to be to look into our own souls and find whether we really want it. In the vast majority of cases we shall find that we are not fit; we do not want; there was no thirst after the spiritual.

There are still more difficulties for the "transmitter". There are many who, though immersed in ignorance, yet, in the pride of their hearts, think they know everything, and not only do not stop there, but offer to take others on their shoulders, and thus "the blind leading the blind, they both fall into the ditch". The world is full of these; everyone wants to be a teacher, every beggar wants to make a gift of a million dollars. Just as the latter is ridiculous, so are these teachers.

How are we to know a teacher then? In the first place, the sun requires no torch to make it visible. We do not light a candle to see the sun. When the sun rises, we instinctively become aware of its rising; and when a teacher of men comes to help us, the soul will instinctively know that it has found the truth. Truth stands on its own evidences; it does not require any other testimony to attest it; it is self-effulgent. It penetrates into the inmost recesses of our nature, and the whole universe stands up and says, "This is Truth." These are the very great teachers, but we can get help from the lesser ones also; and as we ourselves are not always sufficiently intuitive to be certain of our judgment of the man from whom we receive, there ought to be certain tests. There are certain conditions necessary in the taught, and also in the teacher.

The conditions necessary in the taught are purity, a real thirst after knowledge, and perseverance. No impure soul can be religious; that is the one great condition; purity in every way is absolutely necessary. The other condition is a real thirst after knowledge. Who wants ? That is the question. We get whatever we want — that is an old, old law. He who wants, gets. To want religion is a very difficult thing, not so easy as we generally think. Then we always forget that religion does not consist in hearing talks, or in reading books, but it is a continuous struggle, a grappling with our own nature, a continuous fight till the victory is achieved. It is not a question of one or two days, of years, or of lives, but it may be hundreds of lifetimes, and we must be ready for that. It may come immediately, or it may not come in hundreds of lifetimes; and we must be ready for that. The student who sets out with such a spirit finds success.

In the teacher we must first see that he knows the secret of the scriptures. The whole world reads scriptures — Bibles, Vedas, Korans, and others; but they are only words, external arrangement, syntax, the etymology, the philology, the dry bones of religion. The teacher may be able to find what is the age of any book, but words are only the external forms in which things come. Those who deal too much in words and let the mind run always in the force of words lose the spirit. So the teacher must be able to know the spirit of the scriptures. The network of words is like a huge forest in which the human mind loses itself and finds no way out. The various methods of joining words, the various methods of speaking a beautiful language, the various methods of explaining the dicta of the scriptures, are only for the enjoyment of the learned. They do not attain perfection; they are simply desirous to show their learning, so that the world may praise them and see that they are learned men. You will find that no one of the great teachers of the world went into these various explanations of texts; on their part there is no attempt at "text-torturing", no saying, "This word means this, and this is the philological connection between this and that word." You study all the great teachers the world has produced, and you will see that no one of them goes that way. Yet they taught, while others, who have nothing to teach, will take up a word and write a three-volume book on its origin and use. As my Master used to say, what would you think of men who went into a mango orchard and busied themselves in counting the leaves and examining the colour of the leaves, the size of the twigs, the number of branches, and so forth, while only one of them had the sense to begin to eat the mangoes? So leave this counting of leaves and twigs and this note-taking to others. That work has its own value in its proper place, but not here in the spiritual realm. Men never become spiritual through such work; you have never once seen a strong spiritual man among these "leaf-counters". Religion is the highest aim of man, the highest glory, but it does not require "leaf-counting". If you want to be a Christian, it is not necessary to know whether Christ was born in Jerusalem or Bethlehem or just the exact date on which he pronounced the Sermon on the Mount; you only require to feel the Sermon on the Mount. It is not necessary to read two thousand words on when it was delivered. All that is for the enjoyment of the learned. Let them have it; say amen to that. Let us eat the mangoes.

The second condition necessary in the teacher is that he must be sinless. The question was once asked me in England by a friend, "Why should we look to the personality of a teacher? We have only to judge of what he says, and take that up." Not so. If a man wants to teach me something of dynamics or chemistry or any other physical science, he may be of any character; he can still teach dynamics or any other science. For the knowledge that the physical sciences require is simply intellectual and depends on intellectual strength; a man can have in such a case a gigantic intellectual power without the least development of his soul. But in the spiritual sciences it is impossible from first to last that there can be any spiritual light in that soul which is impure. What can such a soul teach? It knows nothing. Spiritual truth is purity. "Blessed are the pure in heart, for they shall see God". In that one sentence is the gist of all religions. If you have learnt that, all that has been said in the past and all that it is possible to say in the future, you have known; you need not look into anything else, for you have all that is necessary in that one sentence; it could save the world, were all the other scriptures lost. A vision of God, a glimpse of the beyond never comes until the soul is pure. Therefore in the teacher of spirituality, purity is the one thing indispensable; we must see first what he is , and then what he says . Not so with intellectual teachers; there we care more for what he says than what he is. With the teacher of religion we must first and foremost see what he is, and then alone comes the value of the words, because he is the transmitter. What will he transmit, if he has not flat spiritual power in him? To give a simile: If a heater is hot, it can convey heat vibrations, but if not, it is impossible to do so. Even so is the case with the mental vibrations of the religious teacher which he conveys to the mind of the taught. It is a question of transference, and not of stimulating only our intellectual faculties. Some power, real and tangible, goes out from the teacher and begins to grow in the mind of the taught. Therefore the necessary condition is that the teacher must be true.

The third condition is motive. We should see that he does not teach with any ulterior motive, for name, or fame, or anything else, but simply for love, pure love for you. When spiritual forces are transmitted from the teacher to the taught, they can only be conveyed through the medium of love; there is no other medium that can convey them. Any other motive, such as gain or name, would immediately destroy the conveying medium; therefore all must be done through love. One who has known God can alone be a teacher. When you see that in the teacher these conditions are fulfilled, you are safe; if they are not fulfilled, it is unwise to accept him. There is a great risk, if he cannot convey goodness, of his conveying wickedness sometimes. This must be guarded against; therefore it naturally follows that we cannot be taught by anybody and everybody.

The preaching of sermons by brooks and stones may be true as a poetical figure but no one can preach a single grain of truth until he has it in himself. To whom do the brooks preach sermons? To that human soul only whose lotus of life has already opened. When the heart has been opened, it can receive teaching from the brooks or the stones — it can get some religious teaching from all these; but the unopened heart will see nothing but brooks and rolling stones. A blind man may come to a museum, but he comes and goes only; if he is to see, his eyes must first be opened. This eye-opener of religion is the teacher. With the teacher, therefore, our relationship is that of ancestor and descendant; the teacher is the spiritual ancestor, and the disciple is the spiritual descendant. It is all very well to talk of liberty and independence, but without humility, submission, veneration, and faith, there will not be any religion. It is a significant fact that where this relation still exists between the teacher and the taught, there alone gigantic spiritual souls grow; but in those who have thrown it off religion is made into a diversion. In nations and churches where this relation between teacher and taught is not maintained spirituality is almost an unknown quantity. It never comes without that feeling; there is no one to transmit and no one to be transmitted to, because they are all independent. Of whom can they learn? And if they come to learn, they come to buy learning. Give me a dollar's worth of religion; cannot I pay a dollar for it? Religion cannot be got that way!

There is nothing higher and holier than the knowledge which comes to the soul transmitted by a spiritual teacher. If a man has become a perfect Yogi it comes by itself, but it cannot be got in books. You may go and knock your head against the four corners of the world, seek in the Himalayas, the Alps, the Caucasus, the Desert of Gobi or Sahara, or the bottom of the sea, but it will not come until you find a teacher. Find the teacher, serve him as a child, open your heart to his influence, see in him God manifested. Our attention should be fixed on the teacher as the highest manifestation of God; and as the power of attention concentrates there, the picture of the teacher as man will melt away; the frame will vanish, and the real God will be left there. Those that come to truth with such we are men. The time will come when we transcend our human nature and know Him as He is; but so long as we are men we must worship Him in man. Talk as we may, try as we may, we cannot see God except as a man. We may deliver great intellectual speeches, become very great rationalists, and prove that these tales of God as all nonsense, but let us come to practical common sense. What is behind this remarkable intellect? Zero, nothing, simply so much froth. When next you hear a man delivering great intellectual lectures against this worship of God, get hold of him and ask him what is his idea of God, what he means by "omnipotence", and "omniscience", and "omnipresent love", and so forth, beyond the spelling of the words. He means nothing, he cannot formulate an idea, he is no better than the man in the street who has not read a single book. That man in the street, however, is quiet and does not disturb the world, while the other man's arguments cause disturbance. He has no actual perception, and both are on the same plane.

Religion is realisation, and you must make the sharpest distinction between talk and realisation. What you perceive in your soul is realisation. Man has no idea of the Spirit, he has to think of it with the forms he has before him. He has to think of the blue skies, or the expansive fields, or the sea, or something huge. How else can you think of God? So what are you doing in reality? You are talking of omnipresence, and thinking of the sea. Is God the sea? A little more common sense is required. Nothing is so uncommon as common sense, the world is too full of talk. A truce to all this frothy argument of the world. We are by our present constitution limited and bound to see God as man. If the buffaloes want to worship God, they will see Him as a huge buffalo. If a fish wants to worship God, it will have to think of Him as a big fish. You and I, the buffalo, the fish, each represents so many different vessels. All these go to the sea to be filled with water a spirit of veneration and love — for them the Lord of truth speaks the most wonderful words. "Take thy shoes from off thy feet, for the place whereon thou standest is holy ground". Wherever His name is spoken, that place is holy. How much more so is a man who speaks His name, and with what veneration ought we to approach a man out of whom come spiritual truths! This is the spirit in which we are to be taught. Such teachers are few in number, no doubt, in this world, but the world is never altogether without them. The moment it is absolutely bereft of these, it will cease to be, it will become a hideous hell and will just drop. These teachers are the fair flowers of human life and keep the world going; it is the strength that is manifested from these hearts of life that keeps the bounds of society intact.

Beyond these is another set of teachers, the Christs of the world. These Teachers of all teachers represent God Himself in the form of man. They are much higher; they can transmit spirituality with a touch, with a wish, which makes even the lowest and most degraded characters saints in one second. Do you not read of how they used to do these things? They are not the teachers about whom I was speaking; they are the Teachers of all teachers, the greatest manifestations of God to man; we cannot see God except through them. We cannot help worshipping them, and they are the only beings we are bound to worship.

No man bath "seen" God but as He is manifested in the Son. We cannot see God. If we try to see Him, we make a hideous caricature of God. There is an Indian story that an ignorant man was asked to make an image of the God Shiva, and after days of struggle he made an image of a monkey. So whenever we attempt to make an image of God, we make a caricature of Him, because we cannot understand Him as anything higher than man so long as according to the shape of each vessel. In each of these vessels is nothing but water. So with God. When men see Him, they see Him as man, and the animals as animal — each according to his ideal. That is the only way you can see Him; you have to worship Him as man, because there is no other way out of it. Two classes of men do not worship God as man — the human brute who has no religion, and the Paramahamsa (highest Yogi) who has gone beyond humanity, who has thrown off his mind and body and gone beyond the limits of nature. All nature has become his Self. He has neither mind nor body, and can worship God as God, as can a Jesus or a Buddha. They did not worship God as man. The other extreme is the human brute. You know how two extremes look alike. Similar is the case with the extreme of ignorance and the other extreme of knowledge; neither of these worships anybody. The extremely ignorant do not worship God, not being developed enough to feel the need for so doing. Those that have attained the highest knowledge also do not worship God — having realised and become one with God. God never worships God. Between these two poles of existence, if anyone tells you he is not going to worship God as man, take care of him. He is an irresponsible talker, he is mistaken; his religion is for frothy thinkers, it is intellectual nonsense.

Therefore it is absolutely necessary to worship God as man, and blessed are those races which have such a "God-man" to worship. Christians have such a God-man in Christ; therefore cling close to Christ; never give up Christ. That is the natural way to see God; see God in man. All our ideas of God are concentrated there. The great limitation Christians have is that they do not heed other manifestations of God besides Christ. He was a manifestation of God; so was Buddha; so were some others, and there will be hundreds of others. Do not limit God anywhere. Pay all the reverence that you think is due to God, to Christ; that is the only worship we can have. God cannot be worshipped; He is the immanent Being of the universe. It is only to His manifestation as man that we can pray. It would be a very good plan, when Christians pray, to say, "in the name of Christ". It would be wise to stop praying to God, and only pray to Christ. God understands human failings and becomes a man to do good to humanity. "Whenever virtue subsides and immorality prevails, then I come to help mankind", says Krishna. He also says, "Fools, not knowing that I, the Omnipotent and Omnipresent God of the universe, have taken this human form, deride Me and think that cannot be." Their minds have been clouded with demoniacal ignorance, so they cannot see in Him the Lord of the universe. These great Incarnations of God are to be worshipped. Not only so, they alone can be worshipped; and on the days of their birth, and on the days when they went out of this world, we ought to pay more particular reverence to them. In worshipping Christ I would rather worship Him just as He desires; on the day of His birth I would rather worship Him by fasting than by feasting — by praying. When these are thought of, these great ones, they manifest themselves in our souls, and they make us like unto them. Our whole nature changes, and we become like them.

But you must not mix up Christ or Buddha with hobgoblins flying through the air and all that sort of nonsense. Sacrilege! Christ coming into a spiritualistic seance to dance! I have seen that presence in this country. It is not in that way that these manifestations of God come. The very touch of one of them will be manifest upon a man; when Christ touches , the whole soul of man will change, that man will be transfigured just as He was. His whole life will be spiritualised; from every pore of his body spiritual power will emanate. What were the great powers of Christ in miracles and healing, in one of his character? They were low, vulgar things that He could not help doing because He was among vulgar beings. Where was this miracle-making done? Among the Jews; and the Jews did not take Him. Where was it not done? In Europe. The miracle-making went to the Jews, who rejected Christ, and the Sermon on the Mount to Europe, which accepted Him. The human spirit took on what was true and rejected what was spurious. The great strength of Christ is not in His miracles or His healing. Any fool could do those things. Fools can heal others, devils can heal others. I have seen horrible demoniacal men do wonderful miracles. They seem to manufacture fruits out of the earth. I have known fools and diabolical men tell the past, present, and future. I have seen fools heal at a glance, by the will, the most horrible diseases. These are powers, truly, but often demoniacal powers. The other is the spiritual power of Christ which will live and always has lived — an almighty, gigantic love, and the words of truth which He preached. The action of healing men at a glance is forgotten, but His saying, "Blessed are the pure in heart", that lives today. These words are a gigantic magazine of power — inexhaustible. So long as the human mind lasts, so long as the name of God is not forgotten, these words will roll on and on and never cease to be. These are the powers Jesus taught, and the powers He had. The power of purity; it is a definite power. So in worshipping Christ, in praying to Him, we must always remember what we are seeking. Not those foolish things of miraculous display, but the wonderful powers of the Spirit, which make man free, give him control over the whole of nature, take from him the badge of slavery, and show God unto him.

THE NEED OF SYMBOLS

Bhakti is divided into two portions. One is called Vaidhi, formal or ceremonial; the other portion is called Mukhyâ, supreme. The word Bhakti covers all the ground between the lowest form of worship and the highest form of life. All the worship that you have seen in any country in the world, or in any religion, is regulated by love. There is a good deal that is simple ceremony; there is also a good deal which, though not ceremony, is still not love, but a lower state. Yet these ceremonies are necessary. The external part of Bhakti is absolutely necessary to help the soul onward. Man makes a great mistake when he thinks that he can at once jump to the highest state. If a baby thinks he is going to be an old man in a day, he is mistaken; and I hope you will always bear in mind this one ideal, that religion is neither in books, nor in intellectual consent, nor in reasoning. Reason, theories, documents, doctrines, books, religious ceremonies, are all helps to religion: religion itself consists in realisation . We all say, "There is a God." Have you seen God? That is the question. You hear a man say, "There is God in heaven." You ask him if he has seen Him, and if he says he has, you would laugh at him and say he is a maniac. With most people religion is a sort of intellectual assent and goes no further than a document. I would not call it religion. It is better to be an atheist than to have that sort of religion. Religion does not depend on our intellectual assent or dissent. You say there is a soul. Have you seen the soul? How is it we all have souls and do not see them? You have to answer the question and find out the way to see the soul. If not, it is useless to talk of religion. If any religion is true, it must be able to show us the soul and show us God and the truth in ourselves. If you and I fight for all eternity about one of these doctrines or documents, we shall never come to any conclusion. People have been fighting for ages, and what is the outcome? Intellect cannot reach there at all. We have to go beyond the intellect; the proof of religion is in direct perception. The proof of the existence of this wall is that we see it; if you sat down and argued about its existence or non-existence for ages, you could never come to any conclusion; but directly you see it, it is enough. If all the men in the world told you it did not exist, you would not believe them, because you know that the evidence of your own eyes is superior to that of all the doctrines and documents in the world.

To be religious, you have first to throw books overboard. The less you read of books, the better for you; do one thing at a time. It is a tendency in Western countries, in these modern times, to make a hotchpotch of the brain; all sorts of unassimilated ideas run riot in the brain and form a chaos without ever obtaining a chance to settle down and crystallise into a definite shape. In many cases it becomes a sort of disease, but this is not religion. Then some want a sensation. Tell them about ghosts and people coming from the North Pole or any other remote place, with wings or in any other form, and that they are invisibly present and watching over them, and make them feel uncanny, then they are satisfied and go home; but within twenty-four hours they are ready for a fresh sensation. This is what some call religion. This is the way to the lunatic asylum, and not to religion. The Lord is not to be reached by the weak, and all these weird things tend to weakness. Therefore go not near them; they only make people weak, bring disorder to the brain, weaken the mind, demoralise the soul, and a hopeless muddle is the result. You must bear in mind that religion does not consist in talk, or doctrines, or books, but in realisation;

it is not learning, but being . Everybody knows, "Do not steal", but what of it? That man has really known who has not stolen. Everybody knows, "Do not injure others", but of what value is it? Those who have not done so have realised it, they know it and have built their character on it. Religion is realising; and I will call you a worshipper of God when you have become able to realise the Idea. Before that it is the spelling of the weird, and no more. It is this power of realisation that makes religion. No amount of doctrines or philosophies or ethical books, that you may have stuffed into your brain, will matter much, only what you are and what you have realised . So we have to realise religion, and this realisation of religion is a long process. When men hear of something very high and wonderful, they all think they will get that, and never stop for a moment to consider that they will have to work their way up to it; they all want to jump there. If it is the highest, we are for it. We never stop to consider whether we have the power, and the result is that we do not do anything. You cannot take a man with a pitchfork and push him up there; we all have to work up gradually. Therefore the first part of religion is Vaidhi Bhakti, the lower phase of worship.

What are these lower phases of worship? They are various. In order to attain to the state where we can realise, we must pass through the concrete — just as you see children learn through the concrete first — and gradually come to the abstract. If you tell a baby that five times two is ten, it will not understand; but if you bring ten things and show how five times two is ten, it will understand. Religion is a long, slow process. We are all of us babies here; we may be old, and have studied all the books in the universe, but we are all spiritual babies. We have learnt the doctrines and dogmas, but realised nothing in our lives. We shall have to begin now in the concrete, through forms and words, prayers and ceremonies; and of these concrete forms there will be thousands; one form need not be for everybody. Some may be helped by images, some may not. Some require an image outside, others one inside the brain. The man who puts it inside says, "I am a superior man. When it is inside it is all right; when it is outside, it is idolatry, I will fight it." When a man puts an image in the form of a church or a temple, he thinks it is holy; but when it is in a human form, he objects to it!

So there are various forms through which the mind will take this concrete exercise; and then, step by step, we shall come to the abstract understanding, abstract realisation. Again, the same form is not for everyone; there is one form that will suit you, and another will suit somebody else, and so on. All forms, though leading to the same goal, may not be for all of us. Here is another mistake we generally make. My ideal does not suit you; and why should I force it on you? My fashion of building churches or reading hymns does not suit you; why should I force it on you? Go into the world and every fool will tell you that his form is the only right one, that every other form is diabolical, and he is the only chosen man ever born in the universe. But in fact, all these forms are good and helpful. Just as there are certain varieties in human nature, so it is necessary that there should be an equal number of forms in religion; and the more there are, the better for the world. If there are twenty forms of religion in the world, it is very good; if there are four hundred, so much the better — there will be the more to choose from. So we should rather be glad when the number of religions and religious ideas increase and multiply, because they will then include every man and help mankind more. Would to God that religions multiplied until every man had his own religion, quite separate from that of any other! This is the idea of the Bhakti-Yogi.

The final idea is that my religion cannot be yours, or yours mine. Although the goal and the aim are the same, yet each one has to take a different road, according to the tendencies of his mind; and although these roads are various, they must all be true, because they lead to the same goal. It cannot be that one is true and the rest not. The choosing of one's own road is called in the language of Bhakti, Ishta, the chosen way.

Then there are words. All of you have heard of the power of words, how wonderful they are! Every book — the Bible, the Koran, and the Vedas — is full of the power of words. Certain words have wonderful power over mankind. Again, there are other forms, known as symbols. Symbols have great influence on the human mind. But great symbols in religion were not created indefinitely. We find that they are the natural expressions of thought. We think symbolically. All our words are but symbols of the thought behind, and different people have come to use different symbols without knowing the reason why. It was all behind, and these symbols are associated with the thoughts; and as the thought brings the symbol outside, so the symbol, on the contrary, can bring the thought inside. So one portion of Bhakti tells about these various subjects of symbols and words and prayers. Every religion has prayers, but one thing you must bear in mind — praying for health or wealth is not Bhakti, it is all Karma or meritorious action. Praying for any physical gain is simply Karma, such as a prayer for going to heaven and so forth. One that wants to love God, to be a Bhakta, must discard all such prayers. He who wants to enter the realms of light must first give up this buying and selling this "shopkeeping" religion, and then enter the gates. It is not that you do not get what you pray for; you get everything, but such praying is a beggar's religion. "Foolish indeed is he who, living on the banks of the Ganga, digs a little well for water. A fool indeed is the man who, coming to a mine of diamonds, seeks for glass beads." This body will die some time, so what is the use of praying for its health again and again? What is there in health and wealth? The wealthiest man can use and enjoy only a little portion of his wealth. We can never get all the things of this world; and if not, who cares? This body will go, who cares for these things? If good things come, welcome; if they go away, let them go. Blessed are they when they come, and blessed are they when they go. We are striving to come into the presence of the King of kings. We cannot get there in a beggar's dress. Even if we wanted to enter the presence of an emperor, should we be admitted? Certainly not. We should be driven out. This is the Emperor of emperors, and in these beggar's rags we cannot enter. Shopkeepers never have admission there; buying and selling have no place there. As you read in the Bible, Jesus drove the buyers and sellers out of the Temple. Do not pray for little things. If you seek only bodily comforts, where is the difference between men and animals? Think yourselves a little higher than that.

So it goes without saying that the first task in becoming a Bhakta is to give up all desires of heaven and other things. The question is how to get rid of these desires. What makes men miserable? Because they are slaves, bound by laws, puppets in the hand of nature, tumbled about like playthings. We are continually taking care of this body that anything can knock down; and so we are living in a constant state of fear. I have read that a deer has to run on the average sixty or seventy miles every day, because it is frightened. We ought to know that we are in a worse plight than the deer. The deer has some rest, but we have none. If the deer gets grass enough it is satisfied, but we are always multiplying our wants. It is a morbid desire with us to multiply our wants. We have become so unhinged and unnatural that nothing natural will satisfy us. We are always grasping after morbid things, must have unnatural excitement — unnatural food, drink, surroundings, and life. As to fear, what are our lives but bundles of fear? The deer has only one class of fear, such as that from tigers, wolves, etc. Man has the whole universe to fear.

How are we to free ourselves from this is the question. Utilitarians say, "Don't talk of God and hereafter; we don't know anything of these things, let us live happily in this world." I would be the first to do so if we could, but the world will not allow us. As long as you are a slave of nature, how can you? The more you struggle, the more enveloped you become. You have been devising plans to make you happy, I do not know for how many years, but each year things seem to grow worse. Two hundred years ago in the old world people had few wants; but if their knowledge increased in arithmetical progression, their wants increased in geometrical progression. We think that in salvation at least our desires will be fulfilled, so we desire to go to heaven. This eternal, unquenchable thirst! Always wanting something! When a man is a beggar, he wants money. When he has money, he wants other things, society; and after that, something else. Never at rest. How are we to quench this? If we get to heaven, it will only increase desire. If a poor man gets rich, it does not quench his desires, it is only like throwing butter on the fire, increasing its bright flames. Going to heaven means becoming intensely richer, and then desire comes more and more. We read of many human things in heaven in the different Bibles of the world; they are not always very good there; and after all, this desire to go to heaven is a desire after enjoyment. This has to be given up. It is too little, too vulgar a thing for you to think of going to heaven. It is just the same as thinking, I will become a millionaire and lord it over people. There are many of these heavens, but through them you cannot gain the right to enter the gates of religion and love.

THE CHIEF SYMBOLS

There are two Sanskrit words, Pratika and Pratimâ. Pratika means coming towards, nearing. In all countries you find various grades of worship. In this country, for instance, there are people who worship images of saints, there are people who worship certain forms and symbols. Then there are people who worship different beings who are higher than men, and their number is increasing very rapidly — worshippers of departed spirits. I read that there are something like eight millions of them here. Then there are other people who worship certain beings of higher grade — the angels, the gods, and so forth. Bhakti-Yoga does not condemn any one of these various grades, but they are all classed under one name, Pratika. These people are not worshipping God, but Pratika, something which is near, a step towards God. This Pratika worship cannot lead us to salvation and freedom; it can only give us certain particular things for which we worship them. For instance, if a man worships his departed ancestors or departed friends, he may get certain powers or certain information from them. Any particular gift that is got from these objects of worship is called Vidyâ, particular knowledge; but freedom, the highest aim, comes only by worship of God Himself. Some Orientalists think, in expounding the Vedas, that even the Personal God Himself is a Pratika. The Personal God may be a Pratika, but the Pratikas are neither the Personal nor Impersonal God. They cannot be worshipped as God. So it would be a great mistake if people thought that by worshipping these different Pratikas, either as angels, or ancestors, or Mahâtmâs (holy men, saints), etc., or departed spirits, they could ever reach to freedom. At best they can only reach to certain powers, but God alone can make us free. But because of that they are not to be condemned, their worship produces some result. The man who does not understand anything higher may get some power, some enjoyment, by the worship of these Pratikas; and after a long course of experience, when he will be ready to come to freedom, he will of his own accord give up the Pratikas.

Of these various Pratikas the most prevalent form is the worship of departed friends. Human nature — personal love, love for our friends — is so strong in us that when they die, we wish to see them once more — clinging on to their forms. We forget that these forms while living were constantly changing, and when they die, we think they become constant, and that we shall see them so. Not only so, but if I have a friend or a son who has been a scoundrel, as soon as he dies, I begin to think he is the saintliest person in existence; he becomes a god. There are people in India who, if a baby dies, do not burn it, but bury it and build a temple over it; and that little baby becomes the god of that temple. This is a very prevalent form of religion in many countries, and there are not wanting philosophers who think this has been the origin of all religions. Of course they cannot prove it. We must remember, however, that this worship of Pratikas can never bring us to salvation or to freedom.

Secondly, it is very dangerous. The danger is that these Pratikas, "nearing-stages", so far as they lead us on to a further stage, are all right; but the chances are ninety-nine to one that we shall stick to the Pratikas all our lives. It is very good to be born in a church, but it is very bad to die there. To make it clearer, it is very good to be born in a certain sect and have its training — it brings out our higher qualities; but in the vast majority of cases we die in that little sect, we never come out or grow. That is the great danger of all these worships of Pratikas. One says that these are all stages which one has to pass, but one never gets out of them; and when one becomes old, one still sticks to them. If a young man does not go to church, he ought to be condemned. But if an old man goes to church, he also ought to be condemned; he has no business with this child's play any more; the church should have been merely a preparation for something higher. What business has he any more with forms and Pratikas and all these preliminaries?

Book worship is another strong form of this Pratika, the strongest form. You find in every country that the book becomes the God. There are sects in my country who believe that God incarnates and becomes man, but even God incarnate as man must conform to the Vedas, and if His teachings do not so conform, they will not take Him. Buddha is worshipped by the Hindus, but if you say to them, "If you worship Buddha, why don't you take His teachings?" they will say, because they, the Buddhists, deny the Vedas. Such is the meaning of book worship. Any number of lies in the name of a religious book are all right. In India if I want to teach anything new, and simply state it on my own authority, as what I think, nobody will come to listen to me; but if I take some passage from the Vedas, and juggle with it, and give it the most impossible meaning, murder everything that is reasonable in it, and bring out my own ideas as the ideas that were meant by the Vedas, all the fools will follow me in a crowd. Then there are men preaching a sort of Christianity that would frighten the ordinary Christian out of his wits; but they say, "This is what Jesus Christ meant", and many come round them. People do not want anything new, if it is not in the Vedas or the Bible It is a case of nerves: when you hear a new and striking thing, you are startled; or when you see a new thing, you are startled; it is constitutional.

It is much more so with thoughts. The mind has been running in ruts, and to take up a new idea is too much of a strain; so the idea has to be put near the ruts, and then we slowly take it. It is a good policy, but bad morality. Think of the mass of incongruities that reformers, and what you call the liberal preachers, pour into society today. According to Christian Scientists, Jesus was a great healer; according to the Spiritualists, He was a great psychic; according to the Theosophists, He was a Mahâtmâ. All these have to be deduced from the same text. There is a text in the Vedas which says, "Existence (Sat) alone existed, O beloved, nothing else existed in the beginning". Many different meanings are given to the word Sat in this text. The Atomists say the word meant "atoms", and out of these atoms the world has been produced. The Naturalists say it meant "nature", and out of nature everything has come. The Shunyavâdins (maintainers of the Void) say it meant "nothing", "zero", and out of nothing everything has been produced. The Theists say it meant "God", and the Advaitists say it was "Absolute Existence", and all refer to the same text as their authority.

These are the defects of book worship. But there is, on the other hand, a great advantage in it: it gives strength. All religious sects have disappeared excepting those that have a book. Nothing seems to kill them. Some of you have heard of the Parsees. They were the ancient Persians, and at one time there were about a hundred millions of them. The majority of them were conquered by the Arabs, and converted to Mohammedanism. A handful fled from their persecutors with their book, which is still preserving them. A book is the most tangible form of God. Think of the Jews; if they had not had a book, they would have simply melted into the world. But that keeps them up; the Talmud keeps them together, in spite of the most horrible persecution. One of the great advantages of a book is that it crystallises everything in tangible and convenient form, and is the handiest of all idols. Just put a book on an altar and everyone sees it; a good book everyone reads. I am afraid I may be considered partial. But, in my opinion books have produced more evil than good. They are accountable for many mischievous doctrines. Creeds all come from books, and books are alone responsible for the persecution and fanaticism in the world. Books in modern times are making liars everywhere. I am astonished at the number of liars abroad in every country.

The next thing to be considered is the Pratima, or image, the use of images. All over the world you will find images in some form or other. With some, it is in the form of a man, which is the best form. If I wanted to worship an image I would rather have it in the form of a man than of an animal, or building, or any other form. One sect thinks a certain form is the right sort of image, and another thinks it is bad. The Christian thinks that when God came in the form of a dove it was all right, but if He comes in the form of a fish, as the Hindus say, it is very wrong and superstitious. The Jews think if an idol be made in the form of a chest with two angels sitting on it, and a book on it, it is all right, but if it is in the form of a man or a woman, it is awful. The Mohammedans think that when they pray, if they try to form a mental image of the temple with the Caaba, the black stone in it, and turn towards the west, it is all right, but if you form the image in the shape of a church it is idolatry. This is the defect of image-worship. Yet all these seem to be necessary stages.

In this matter it is of supreme importance to think what we ourselves believe. What we have realised, is the question. What Jesus, or Buddha, or Moses did is nothing to us, unless we too do it for ourselves. It would not satisfy our hunger to shut ourselves up in a room and think of what Moses ate, nor would what Moses thought save us . My ideas are very radical on these points. Sometimes I think that I am right when I agree with all the ancient teachers, at other times I think they are right when they agree with me. I believe in thinking independently. I believe in becoming entirely free from the holy teachers; pay all reverence to them, but look at religion as an independent research. I have to find my light, just as they found theirs. Their finding the light will not satisfy us at all. You have to become the Bible, and not to follow it, excepting as paying reverence to it as a light on the way, as a guide-post, a mark: that is all the value it has. But these images and other things are quite necessary. You may try to concentrate your mind, or even to project any thought. You will find that you naturally form images in your mind. You cannot help it. Two sorts of persons never require any image — the human animal who never thinks of any religion, and the perfected being who has passed through these stages. Between these two points all of us require some sort of ideal, outside and inside. It may be in the form of a departed human being, or of a living man or woman. This is clinging to personality and bodies, and is quite natural. We are prone to concretise. How could we be here if we did not concretise? We are concreted spirits, and so we find ourselves here on this earth. Concretisation has brought us here, and it will take us out. Going after things of the senses has made us human beings, and we are bound to worship personal beings, whatever we may say to the contrary. It is very easy to say "Don't be personal"; but the same man who says so is generally most personal. His attachment for particular men and women is very strong; it does not leave him when they die, he wants to follow them beyond death. That is idolatry; it is the seed, the very cause of idolatry; and the cause being there it will come out in some form. Is it not better to have a personal attachment to an image of Christ or Buddha than to an ordinary man or woman? In the West, people say that it is bad to kneel before images, but they can kneel before a woman and say, "You are my life, the light of my eyes, my soul." That is worse idolatry. What ifs this talk about my soul my life? It will soon go away. It is only sense-attachment. It is selfish love covered by a mass of flowers. Poets give it a good name and throw lavender-water and all sorts of attractive things over it. Is it not better to kneel before a statue of Buddha or the Jina conqueror and say, "Thou art my life"? I would rather do that.

There is another sort of Pratika which is not recognised in Western countries, bout is taught in our books. This teaches the worship of mind as God. Anything that is worshipped as God is a stage, a nearing, as it were. An example of this is the method of showing the fine star known as Arundhati, near the group Pleiades. One is shown a big star near to it, and when he has fixed his attention on this and has come to know it, he is shown a finer and still nearer star; and when he has fixed his attention on that, he is led up to Arundhati. So all these various Pratikas and Pratimas lead to God. The worship of Buddha and of Christ constitute a Pratika. a drawing near to the worship of God. But this worship of Buddha and of Christ will not save a man, he must go beyond them to Him who manifested Himself as Jesus Christ, for God alone can give us freedom. There are even some philosophers who say these should he regarded as God; they are not Pratikas, but God Himself. However, we can take all these different Pratikas, these different stages of approach, and not be hurt by them: but if we think while we are worshipping them that we are worshipping God, we are mistaken. If a man worships Jesus Christ, and thinks he will be saved by that, he is mistaken entirely. If a man thinks that by worshipping an idol or the ghosts or spirits of the departed he will be saved, he is entirely mistaken. We may worship anything by seeing God in it, if we can forget the idol and see God there. We must not project any image upon God. But we may fill any image with that Life which is God. Only forget the image, and you are right enough — for "Out of Him comes everything". He is everything. We may worship a picture as God, but not God as the picture. God in the picture is right, but the picture as God is wrong. God in the image is perfectly right. There is no danger there. This is the real worship of God. But the image-God is a mere Pratika.

The next great thing to consider in Bhakti is the "word", the Nâmashakti, the power of the name. The whole universe is composed of name and form. Whatever we see is either a compound of name and form, or simply name with form which is a mental image. So, after all, there is nothing that is not name and form. We all believe God to be without form or shape, but as soon as we begin to think of Him, He acquires both name and form The Chitta is like the calm lake, thoughts being like waves upon this Chitta — and name and form are the normal ways in which these waves arise; no wave can rise without name and form. The uniform cannot be thought of; it is beyond thought; as soon as it becomes thought and matter, it must have name and form. We cannot separate these. It is said in many books that God created the universe out of the Word. Shabdabrahman, in Sanskrit, is the Christian theory of the Word. An old Indian theory, it was taken to Alexandria by Indian preachers and was planted there. Thus the idea of the Word and the Incarnation became fixed there.

There is deep meaning in the thought that God created everything out of the Word. God Himself being formless, this is the best way to describe the projection of forms, or the creation. The Sanskrit word for creation is Srishti, projection. What is meant by "God created things out of nothing"? The universe is projected out of God. He becomes the universe, and it all returns to Him, and again it proceeds forth, and again returns. Through all eternity it will go on in that way. We have seen that the projection of anything in the mind cannot be without name and form. Suppose the mind to be perfectly calm, entirely without thought; nevertheless, as soon as thought begins to rise it will immediately take name and form. Every thought has a certain name and a certain form. In the same way the very fact of creation, the very fact of projection is eternally connected with name and form. Thus we find that every idea that man has, or can have, must be connected with a certain name or word as its counterpart. This being so, it is quite natural to suppose that this universe is the outcome of mind, just as your body is the outcome of your idea — your idea, as it were, made concrete and externalised. If it be true, moreover, that the whole universe is built on the same plan, then, if you know the manner in which one atom is built, you can understand how the whole universe is built. If it is true that in you, the body forms the gross part outside and the mind forms the fine part inside, and both are eternally inseparable, then, when you cease to have the body, you will cease to have the mind also. When a man's brain is disturbed, his ideas also get disturbed, because they are but one, the finer and the grosser parts. There are not two such things as matter and mind. As in a high column of air there are dense and rarefied strata of one and the same element air, so it is with the body; it is one thing throughout, layer on layer, from grosser to finer. Again, the body is like the finger nails. As these continue growing even when they are cut, so from our subtle ideas grows body after body. The finer a thing the more persistent it is; we find that always. The grosser it is the less persistent. Thus, form is the grosser and name the finer state of a single manifesting power called thought. But these three are one; it is the Unity and the Trinity, the three degrees of existence of the same thing. Finer, more condensed, and most condensed. Wherever the one is, the others are there also. Wherever name is, there is form and thought.

It naturally follows that if the universe is built upon the same plan as the body, the universe also must have the same divisions of form, name, and thought. The "thought" is the finest part of the universe, the real motive power. The thought behind our body is called soul, and the thought behind the universe is called God. Then after that is the name, and last of all is the form which we see and feel. For instance, you are a particular person, a little universe in this universe, a body with a particular form; then behind that a name, John or Jane, and behind that again a thought; similarly there is this whole universe, and behind that is the name, what is called the "Word" in all religions, and behind that is God. The universal thought is Mahat, as the Sânkhyas call it, universal consciousness. What is that name? There must be some name. The world is homogeneous, and modern science shows beyond doubt that each atom is composed of the same material as the whole universe. If you know one lump of clay you know the whole universe. Man is the most representative being in the universe, the microcosm, a small universe in himself. So in man we find there is the form, behind that the name, and behind that the thought, the thinking being. So this universe must be on exactly the same plan. The question is: What is that name? According to the Hindus that word is Om. The old Egyptians also believed that. The Katha Upanishad says, "That, seeking which a man practices Brahmacharya, I will tell you in short what that is, that is Om. ... This is Brahman, the Immutable One, and is the highest; knowing this Immutable One, whatever one desires one gets."

This Om stands for the name of the whole universe, or God. Standing midway between the external world and God, it represents both. But then we can take the universe piecemeal, according to the different senses, as touch, as colour, as taste, and in various other ways. In each case we can make of this universe millions of universes from different standpoints, each of which will be a complete universe by itself, and each one will have a name, and a form, and a thought behind. These thoughts behind are Pratikas. Each of them has a name. These names of sacred symbols are used in Bhakti-Yoga. They have almost infinite power. Simply by repetition of these words we can get anything we desire, we can come to perfection. But two things are necessary. "The teacher must be wonderful, so also must be the taught", says the Katha Upanishad. Such a name must come from a person to whom it has descended through right succession. From master to disciple, the spiritual current has been coming; from ancient times, bearing its power. The person from whom such a word comes is called a Guru, and the person to whom it goes is called Shishya, the disciple. When the word has been received in the regular way, and when it has been repeated, much advance has been made in Bhakti-Yoga. Simply by the repetition of that word will come even the highest state of Bhakti. "Thou hast so many names. Thou understandest what is meant by them all these names are Thine, and in each is Thine infinite power; there is neither time nor place for repeating these names, for all times and places are holy. Thou art so easy, Thou art so merciful, how unfortunate am I, that I have no love for Thee!"

THE ISHTA

The theory of Ishta, which I briefly referred to before, is a subject requiring careful attention because with a proper understanding of this, all the various religions of the world can be understood. The word Ishta is derived from the root Ish, to desire, choose. The ideal of all religions, all sects, is the same — the attaining of liberty and cessation of misery. Wherever you find religion, you find this ideal working in one form or other. Of course in lower stages of religion it is not so well expressed; but still, well or ill-expressed, it is the one goal to which every religion approaches. All of us want to get rid of misery; we are struggling to attain to liberty — physical, mental, spiritual. This is the whole idea upon which the world is working. Through the goal is one and the same, there may be many ways to reach it, and these ways are determined by the peculiarities of our nature. One man's nature is emotional, another's intellectual, another's active, and so forth. Again, in the same nature there may be many subdivisions. Take for instance love, with which we are specially concerned in this subject of Bhakti. One man's nature has a stronger love for children; another has it for wife, another for mother, another for father, another for friends. Another by nature has love for country, and a few love humanity in the broadest sense; they are of course very few, although everyone of us talks of it as if it were the guiding motive power of our lives. Some few sages have experienced it. A few great souls among mankind feel this universal love, and let us hope that this world will never be without such men.

We find that even in one subject there are so many different ways of attaining to its goal. All Christians believe in Christ; but think, how many different explanations they have of him. Each church sees him in a different light, from different standpoints. The Presbyterian's eyes are fixed upon that scene in Christ's life when he went to the money-changers; he looks on him as a fighter. If you ask a Quaker, perhaps he will say, "He forgave his enemies." The Quaker takes that view, and so on. If you ask a Roman Catholic, what point of Christ's life is the most pleasing to him, he, perhaps, will say, "When he gave the keys to Peter". Each sect is bound to see him in its own way.

It follows that there will be many divisions and subdivisions even of the same subject. Ignorant persons take one of these subdivisions and take their stand upon it, and they not only deny the right of every other man to interpret the universe according to his own light, but dare to say that others are entirely wrong, and they alone are right. If they are opposed, they begin to fight. They say that they will kill any man who does not believe as they believe, just as the Mohammedans do. These are people who think they are sincere, and who ignore all others. But what is the position we want to take in this Bhakti-Yoga? Not only that we would not tell others that they are wrong, but that we would tell them that they are right — all of these who follow their own ways. That way, which your nature makes it absolutely necessary for you to take, is the right way. Each one of us is born with a peculiarity of nature as the result of our past existence. Either we call it our own reincarnated past experience or a hereditary past; whatever way we may put it, we are the result of the past - that is absolutely certain, through whatever channels that past may have come. It naturally follows that each one of us is an effect, of which our past has been the cause; and as such, there is a peculiar movement, a peculiar train, in each one of us; and therefore each one will have to find way for himself.

This way, this method, to which each of us is naturally adapted, is called the "chosen way". This is the theory of Ishta, and that way which is ours we call our own Ishta. For instance, one man's idea of God is that He is the omnipotent Ruler of the universe. His nature is perhaps such. He is an overbearing man who wants to rule everyone; he naturally finds God an omnipotent Ruler. Another man, who was perhaps a schoolmaster, and severe, cannot see any but a just God, a God of punishment, and so on Each one sees God according to his own nature; and this vision, conditioned by our own nature, is our Ishta. We have brought ourselves to a position where we can see that vision of God, and that alone; we cannot see any other vision. You will perhaps sometimes think of the teaching of a man that it is the best and fits you exactly, and the next day you ask one of your friends to go and hear him; but he comes away with the idea that it was the worst teaching he had ever heard. He is not wrong, and it is useless to quarrel with him. The teaching was all right, but it was not fitted to that man. To extend it a little further, we must understand that truth seen from different standpoints can be truth, and yet not the same truth.

This would seem at first to be a contradiction in terms, but we must remember that an absolute truth is only one, while relative truths are necessarily various. Take your vision of this universe, for instance. This universe, as an absolute entity, is unchangeable, and unchanged, and the same throughout. But you and I and everybody else hear and see, each one his own universe. Take the sun. The sun is one; but when you and I and a hundred other people stand at different places and look at it, each one of us sees a different sun. We cannot help it. A very little change of place will change a man's whole vision of the sun. A slight change in the atmosphere will make again a different vision. So, in relative perception, truth always appears various. But the Absolute Truth is only one. Therefore we need not fight with others when we find they; are telling something about religion which is not exactly according to our view of it. We ought to remember that both of us may be true, though apparently contradictors. There may be millions of radii converging towards the same centre in the sun. The further they are from the centre, the greater is the distance between any two. But as they all meet at the centre, all difference vanishes. There is such a centre, which is the absolute goal of mankind. It is God. We are the radii. The distances between the radii are the constitutional limitations through which alone we can catch the vision of God. While standing on this plane, we are bound each one of us to have a different view of the Absolute Reality; and as such, all views are true, and no one of us need quarrel with another. The only solution lies in approaching the centre. If we try to settle our differences by argument or quarrelling, we shall find that we can go on for hundreds of years without coming to a conclusion. History proves that. The only solution is to march ahead and go towards the centre; and the sooner we do that the sooner our differences will vanish.

This theory of Ishta, therefore, means allowing a man to choose his own religion. One man should not force another to worship what he worships. All attempts to herd together human beings by means of armies, force, or arguments, to drive them pell-mell into the same enclosure and make them worship the same God have failed and will fail always, because it is constitutionally impossible to do so. Not only so, there is the danger of arresting their growth. You scarcely meet any man or woman who is not struggling for some sort of religion; and how many are satisfied, or rather how few are satisfied! How few find anything! And why? Simply because most of them go after impossible tasks. They are forced into these by the dictation of others. For instance, when I am a child, my father puts a book into my hand which says God is such and such. What business has he to put that into my mind? How does he know what way I would develop? And being ignorant of my constitutional development, he wants to force his ideas on my brain, with the result that my growth is stunted. You cannot make a plant grow in soil unsuited to it. A child teaches itself. But you can help it to go forward in its own way. What you can do is not of the positive nature, but of the negative. You can take away the obstacles, but knowledge comes out of its own nature. Loosen the soil a little, so that it may come out easily. Put a hedge round it; see that it is not killed by anything, and there your work stops. You cannot do anything else. The rest is a manifestation from within its own nature. So with the education of a child; a child educates itself. You come to hear me, and when you go home, compare what you have learnt, and you will find you have thought out the same thing; I have only given it expression. I can never teach you anything: you will have to teach yourself, but I can help you perhaps in giving expression to that thought.

So in religion — more so — I must teach myself religion. What right has my father to put all sorts of nonsense into my head? What right has my master or society to put things into my head? Perhaps they are good, but they may not be my way. Think of the appalling evil that is in the world today, of the millions and millions of innocent children perverted by wrong ways of teaching. How many beautiful things which would have become wonderful spiritual truths have been nipped in the bud by this horrible idea of a family religion, a social religion, a national religion, and so forth. Think of what a mass of superstition is in your head just now about your childhood's religion, or your country's religion, and what an amount of evil it does, or can do. Man does not know what a potent power lies behind each thought and action. The old saying is true that, "Fools rush in where angels fear to tread." This should be kept in view from the very first. How? By this belief in Ishta. There are so many ideals; I have no right to say what shall be your ideal, to force any ideal on you. My duty should be to lay before you all the ideals I know of and enable you to see by your own constitution what you like best, and which is most fitted to you. Take up that one which suits you best and persevere in it. This is your Ishta, your special ideal.

We see then that a congregational religion can never be. The real work of religion must be one's own concern. I have an idea of my own, I must keep it sacred and secret, because I know that it need not be your idea. Secondly, why should I create a disturbance by wanting to tell everyone what my idea is? Other people would come and fight me. They cannot do so if I do not tell them; but if I go about telling them what my ideas are, they will all oppose me. So what is the use of talking about them? This Ishta should be kept secret, it is between you and God. All theoretical portions of religion can be preached in public and made congregational, but higher religion cannot be made public. I cannot get ready my religious feelings at a moment's notice. What is the result of this mummery and mockery? It is making a joke of religion, the worst of blasphemy. The result is what you find in the churches of the present day. How can human beings stand this religious drilling? It is like soldiers in a barrack. Shoulder arms, kneel down, take a book, all regulated exactly. Five minutes of feeling, five minutes of reason, five minutes of prayer, all arranged beforehand. These mummeries have driven out religion. Let the churches preach doctrines, theories, philosophies to their hearts'

content, but when it comes to worship, the real practical part of religion, it should be as Jesus says, "When thou prayest, enter into thy closet, and when thou hast shut thy door, pray to thy Father which is in secret"

This is the theory of Ishta. It is the only way to make religion meet practically the necessities of different constitutions, to avoid quarrelling with others, and to make real practical progress in spiritual life. But I must warn you that you do not misconstrue my words into the formation of secret societies. If there were a devil, I would look for him within a secret society — as the invention of secret societies. They are diabolical schemes. The Ishta is sacred , not secret. But in what sense? Why should I not speak of my Ishta to others? Because it is my own most holy thing. It may help others, but how do I know that it will not rather hurt them? There may be a man whose nature is such that he cannot worship a Personal God, but can only worship as an Impersonal God his own highest Self. Suppose I leave him among you, and he tells you that there is no Personal God, but only God as the Self in you or me. You will be shocked. His idea is sacred, but not secret. There never was a great religion or a great teacher that formed secret societies to preach God's truths. There are no such secret societies in India. Such things are purely Western in idea, and merely foisted upon India. We never knew anything about them. Why indeed should there be secret societies in India? In Europe, people were not allowed to talk a word about religion that did not agree with the views of the Church. So they were forced to go about amongst the mountains in hiding and form secret societies, that they might follow their own kind of worship. There was never a time in India when a man was persecuted for holding his own views on religion. There were never secret religious societies in India, so any idea of that sort you must give up at once. These secret societies always degenerate into the most horrible things. I have seen enough of this world to know what evil they cause, and how easily they slide into free love societies and ghost societies, how men play into the hands of other men or women, and how their future possibilities of growth in thought and act are destroyed, and so on. Some of you may be displeased with me for talking in this way, but I must tell you the truth. Perhaps only half a dozen men and women will follow me in all my life; but they will be real men and women, pure and sincere, and I do not want a crowd. What can crowds do? The history of the world was made by a few dozens, whom you can count on your fingers, and the rest were a rabble. All these secret societies and humbugs make men and women impure, weak and narrow; and the weak have no will, and can never work. Therefore have nothing to do with them. All this false love of mystery should be knocked on the head the first time it comes into your mind. No one who is the least impure will ever become religious. Do not try to cover festering sores with masses of roses. Do you think you can cheat God? None can. Give me a straightforward man or woman; but Lord save me from ghosts, flying angels, and devils. Be common, everyday, nice people.

There is such a thing as instinct in us, which we have in common with the animals, a reflex mechanical movement of the body. There is again a higher form of guidance, which we call reason, when the intellect obtains facts and then generalises them. There is a still higher form of knowledge which we call inspiration, which does not reason, but knows things by flashes. That is the highest form of knowledge. But how shall we know it from instinct? That is the great difficulty. Everyone comes to you, nowadays, and says he is inspired, and puts forth superhuman claims. How are we to distinguish between inspiration and deception? In the first place, inspiration must not contradict reason. The old man does not contradict the child, he is the development of the child. What we call inspiration is the development of reason. The way to intuition is through reason. Instinctive movements of your body do not oppose reason. As you cross a street, how instinctively you move your body to save yourself from the cars. Does your mind tell you it was foolish to save your body that way? It does not. Similarly, no genuine inspiration ever contradicts reason. Where it does it is no inspiration. Secondly, inspiration must be for the good of one and all, and not for name or fame, or personal gain. It should always be for the good of the world, and perfectly unselfish. When these tests are fulfilled, you are quite safe to take it as inspiration. You must remember that there is not one in a million that is inspired, in the present state of the world. I hope their number will increase. We are now only playing with religion. With inspiration we shall begin to have religion. Just as St. Paul says, "For now we see through a glass darkly, but then face to face." But in the present state of the world they are few and far between who attain to that state; yet perhaps at no other period were such false claims made to inspiration, as now. It is said that women have intuitive faculties, while men drag themselves slowly upward by reason. Do not believe it. There are just as many inspired men as women, though women have perhaps more claim to peculiar forms of hysteria and nervousness. You had better die as an unbeliever than be played upon by cheats and jugglers. The power of reasoning was given you for use. Show then that you have used it properly. Doing so, you will be able to take care of higher things.

We must always remember that God is Love. "A fool indeed is he who, living on the banks of the Ganga, seeks to dig a little well for water. A fool indeed is the man who, living near a mine of diamonds, spends his life in searching for beads of glass." God is that mine of diamonds. We are fools indeed to give up God for legends of ghosts or flying hobgoblins. It is a disease, a morbid desire. It degenerates the race, weakens the nerves and the brain, living in incessant morbid fear of hobgoblins, or stimulating the hunger for wonders; all these wild stories about them keep the nerves at an unnatural tension — a slow and sure degeneration of the race. It is degeneration to think of giving up God, purity, holiness, and spirituality, to go after all this nonsense! Reading other men's thoughts! If I must read everyone else's thoughts for five minutes at a time I shall go crazy. Be strong and stand up and seek the God of Love. This is the highest strength. What power is higher than the power of purity? Love and purity govern the world. This love of God cannot be reached by the weak; therefore, be not weak, either physically, mentally, morally or spiritually. The Lord alone is true. Everything else is untrue; everything else should be rejected for the salve of the Lord. Vanity of vanities, all is vanity. Serve the Lord and Him alone.

The mission of the Institute of Thought and Philosophy is to preserve and propagate the teachings of Swami Vivekananda. This great Indian spiritual leader is known for introducing the West to Hinduism. Drawing from his vast literary legacy, we provide valuable insights and practical guidance for modern living.

Have any query or feedback? Please reach out to us at

ITPPress123@gmail.com

Wedding Pickle

Neha Sharma hails from Bangalore, the garden city of India, and was born in New Delhi. She is a defense kid; having traveled nearly the whole of India. She holds a Master's degree in HR and International Business.

Neha moved to Norway in 2010 after her wedding and has been there since. She is a mother to a three-year-old. She loves to sit for hours weaving stories about people from different walks of life. She loves to give life to different characters and tell stories to people that can bring out a message or just touch their hearts. Her friends call her a day dreamer as she likes being lost in her own world of imagination where nearly everything seems possible.

Neha has a blog - www.inkedemotions.com which consists of short stories, they mostly speak of the strength of the women in our country.